W9-ASG-010

JOBS

THE STATE *of* **BLACK AMERICA**®

2010: Responding to the Crisis

A
NATIONAL URBAN LEAGUE
PUBLICATION

Library of Congress Control Number:
77-647469

ISBN-0-914758-04-7

EAN: 9780914758020

THE STATE OF BLACK AMERICA 2010

JOBS: RESPONDING TO THE CRISIS

Editor-in-Chief
Stephanie J. Jones

Managing Editor
Valerie Rawlston Wilson

Managing/Creative Directors
Amber C. Jaynes
Rhonda Spears Bell

Associate Editor
Lisa Bland Malone

Editorial Assistant
Clarissa McKithen

Design
Untuck Design Studio

Photography (COVER)
North Park Studios

INDEX

PLAN

GREEN

I

II

III

IV

V

VI

VII

VIII

IX

CONTENTS

From the President's Desk

MARC H. MORIAL
PRESIDENT & CEO, NATIONAL URBAN LEAGUE

 This year we witnessed in horror of the devastation caused by an earthquake in Haiti. The overwhelming lesson of the devastation is that poverty and a broken safety net amplify despair a thousand times over in the event of a natural disaster. Hurricane Katrina, which ravaged New Orleans less than five years ago, showed us here in our own country the duty of a government to safeguard its citizens.

As we examine the state of Black America in 2010, the nation has just begun to recover from another devastation: one of the worst economic crises in its history, a crisis that threatens us just as surely as any hurricane or earthquake. Left in its wake is a near-record high unemployment rate for African Americans that threatens to push an already-struggling community deeper into poverty and despair. The nation's response must be as urgent.

In January of this year, the unemployment rate for African Americans was 16.5%, almost twice the white unemployment rate. Younger men have been hit especially hard, with about 1 in five African American men aged 20 to 24 out of work.

This edition of *The State of Black America* marks the National Urban League's 100th year. As part of our Centennial observation, we have launched a national initiative to address education, housing, health care and employment. At this moment in history, the most urgent of these unquestionably is employment.

Whitney M. Young, who guided the National Urban League through the landmark civil rights struggles of the 1960s, said, "The hardest work in the world is being out of work." A recent *New York Times* poll showed that the trauma of joblessness affects people not just financially, but emotionally and physically. Unemployment is linked to clinical anxiety and depression, alienation from family and friends, and health problems exacerbated by a lack of health insurance and inability to afford medical care.

This edition of *The State of Black America* responds to this crisis. It presents the National Urban League's Plan for Creating Jobs and features analysis and recommendations from experts and leaders who outline specific steps to address the employment crisis in urban communities. The relationships between jobs and education, healthcare, broadband access and environmentalism are also examined in-depth. The data and analysis included in this report all reinforce the need for our recommendations to be included in a federal jobs plan as soon as possible so we can stem the tide of joblessness threatening our cities.

Recently, other civil rights leaders and I met with President Obama to discuss specific action that must happen on the federal level in order to address the employment crisis. We asked for a jobs initiative targeted to urban America and communities where unemployment is highest. The United States needs federal legislation that includes a stronger focus on job training, tax incentives for job creation, extension of unemployment benefits and direct public sector jobs. This nation's urban areas are the economic engines of our economy.

The unemployment rate for African Americans was 16.5%, almost twice the white unemployment rate.

During my meeting with President Obama, I found him to be sensitive to the challenges facing urban communities. Economic experts agree that his leadership over the last year, including the passage of a $787 billion stimulus package, has staved off a greater catastrophe and probably saved as many as 2 million jobs. There is reason for hope, but much, much more must be done.

The occasion of the National Urban League's Centennial is a time not just for reflecting on our legacy, but looking forward to the challenges ahead. *The State of Black America* can serve as a roadmap for that journey.

100

I Am Empowered!

This year the National Urban League celebrates 100 years at the forefront of the civil rights movement. Since its inception in 1910, the National Urban League has been steadfast in its commitment to empowering communities and changing lives.

Today, with key programs focused on eliminating the equality gap for African Americans and all people, the National Urban League delivers social services and programs to over two million people annually through a network of nearly 100 affiliates.

The Centennial celebration is a time to reflect on the rich history and legacy of the National Urban League. With a proven track record of pulling people out of poverty and putting them on the path to empowerment, the National Urban League celebrates its centennial by launching the I AM EMPOWERED campaign.

Focused on four aspirational goals for America in the areas of education, employment, housing and healthcare, I AM EMPOWERED is galvanizing people across the country to take a pledge to commit their time and talent to help achieve the following goals by 2025:

» *Every American child is ready for college, work and life.*

» *Every American has access to jobs with a living wage and good benefits.*

» *Every American lives in safe, decent, affordable and energy-efficient housing on fair terms.*

» *Every American has access to quality and affordable health care solutions.*

Highlighting the employment crisis in urban centers, this year's *State of Black America* report is an important guide to reaching the lofty goal: "Every American has access to jobs with a living wage and good benefits." In these pages you will find innovative and crucial information and data to help the country on the road to an empowered future.

Take the I AM EMPOWERED pledge today and join the growing number of people across the country committed to building a better future and empowering the nation!

Take the pledge today @ *www.iamempowered.com.*

Introduction to the 2010 Equality Index™

VALERIE RAWLSTON WILSON, PH.D.
NATIONAL URBAN LEAGUE POLICY INSTITUTE

The year 2010 is shaping up to be a significant year in American history for a number of reasons. First, 2010 will likely mark the end of the greatest economic downturn the nation has experienced since the Great Depression. That brings us to a crossroads in terms of mapping out a plan for economic recovery and establishing the course of the United States economy for generations to come. Second, the National Urban League celebrates 100 years of dedication to the dual mission of fighting for civil rights and economic empowerment for historically underserved urban communities. Third, the 23rd decennial United States Census will be taking place this year. With expectations that at least one-third of those counted will be non-white, the 2010 Census stands in stark contrast to the first Census in 1790 when blacks were only counted as ⅗ of a person and not even listed by name.

Together these three seemingly unrelated events have been appointed to intersect at this place in time to raise some very important questions. What role will the demographic shift in the nation's population have on our economic future? Can we really afford to craft a recovery and job creation plan that leaves large segments of the African American and Hispanic communities behind? Is the mission of the National Urban League as important now as it was 100 years ago? As we examine this year's Equality Index, which in addition to the usual black-white comparison also includes a first time Hispanic-white comparison, let's consider what the facts reported in the following pages have to say about the answers to these questions.

INTERPRETING THE EQUALITY INDEX

The Equality Index can be interpreted as the relative status of blacks and whites in American society, measured according to five areas—economics, health, education, social justice and civic engagement.

For any given measure, the index represents the ratio of blacks to whites.[1] To use median household income as an example, an index of 62% = $34,218/$55,530, where $34,218 is the median household income for blacks and $55,530 is the median household income for whites. Equality would be indicated by an index of 100%. Therefore, an Equality Index less than 100% suggests that blacks are doing worse relative to whites, and an Equality Index greater than 100% suggests that blacks are doing better than whites.

The overall Equality Index is a weighted average of indices calculated for each of the five sub-categories—economics, health, education, social justice and civic engagement. In turn, the indices for each of the five sub-categories are themselves weighted averages of indices calculated from individual variables (like the example of median household income used above) available from nationally representative data sources. The appropriate data sources and data years are indicated in the accompanying tables at the end of this chapter.

What's New in the 2010 Equality Index?

The 2010 Equality Index stands at 71.8% compared to a revised 2009 index of 71.2%. Revisions to the previous year's index are done for greater comparability across years and reflect data points that have been corrected,

The 2010 Equality Index stands at 71.8%

removed from the current year's index or re-weighted so that less emphasis is placed on older data. The 0.6 percentage point increase in this year's overall index represents the first one-year uptick in the index in the last four years. While at first glance this seems like good news, it must be tempered by the fact that due to minimal changes in four of the five sub-categories, most of the change in this year's index is being driven by the 4.6 percentage points increase in the civic engagement index (from 97.6% to 102.2%). The score improved primarily because of the large increase in black voter turnout during the 2008 election season.

Progress in the other four areas is as follows. Social justice (from 57.2% to 57.1%) and economics (unchanged at 57.4%) top the list of categories exhibiting the greatest degree of inequality, followed by health (from 76.8% to 77.0%) and then education (from 77.0% to 77.6%). The fact that the social justice and economics indices were much closer this year than in previous years is more reflective of changes in the Bureau of Justice Statistics' method of reporting and the resulting re-weighting of available data points than of actual changes in conditions. Also, the lack of change between the revised 2009 and 2010 social justice index can be attributed to the fact that new data for some of the more heavily weighted components of the index were not available this year. A comparison of the revised 2009 and 2010 Equality Index is shown in *Figure 1*.

Figure 1: *Change in Equality Index, 2009-2010*

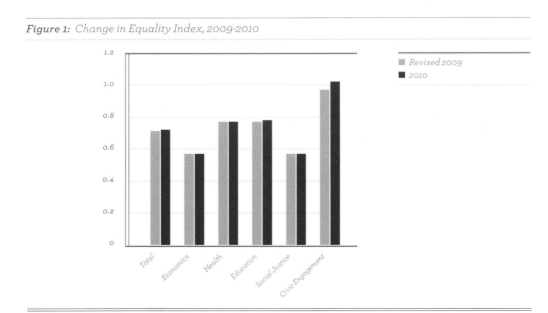

Introducing the Equality Index
of Hispanic America

The biggest change this year is the addition of a Hispanic Equality Index which has been included to expand the discussion of inequality in America to reflect the shifting demographics of this country. The Hispanic Equality Index was calculated similarly to the Equality Index of Black America, except that several data points used to calculate the black-white index were not available for Hispanics. In order to compensate for this, weights were redistributed among the

available variables and a comparable black-white index was calculated using only data available for all three groups—blacks, whites & Hispanics—

so that a consistent comparison can be made. For the purpose of this section's analysis only, the *comparable black-white index* is the appropriate tool. However, the *comparable black-white index* is only intended as a means of comparing equality across all three groups and is in no way a substitute for the original Equality Index of Black America as it relates to direct analysis of black-white inequality.

The 2010 Hispanic Equality Index stands at 75.5%. Across each of the five categories, the sub-indices are as follows: economics 61%, social justice 62.4%, civic engagement 71.9%, education 76.5% and health 103.4%. *Figure 2* provides a comparison of the hispanic-white index and the comparable black-white index.

The patterns of inequality for blacks and Hispanics relative to their white counterparts are similar in some ways, yet quite different in others. For example, for both groups, economics and social justice are the two areas of greatest

The 2010 Hispanic Equality Index stands at 75.5%.

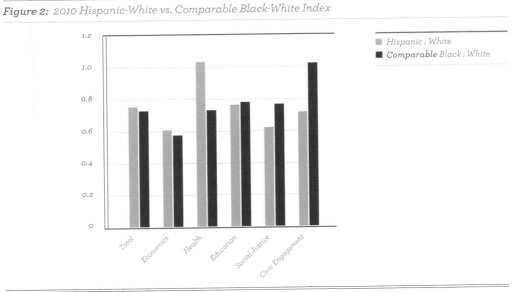

Figure 2: *2010 Hispanic-White vs. Comparable Black-White Index*

Legend:
- Hispanic : White
- **Comparable** Black : White

(Categories: Total, Economics, Health, Education, Social Justice, Civic Engagement)

inequality. However, whereas blacks are most equal to whites in the area of civic engagement (102.2% for blacks compared to 71.9% for Hispanics), Hispanics are most equal in the area of health (103.4% for Hispanics compared to 72.9% for blacks). When we look at the data behind these indices, some of the reasons for the differences become clearer. In the area of civic engagement, black voter registration and participation surpasses that of their Hispanic counterparts by 10.3 and 14.8 percentage points, respectively. And in terms of health, death rates (for all causes) among blacks exceed those of Hispanics by 56 percent. The following section further discusses some of the key statistics behind the Equality Index of Black America and the Equality Index of Hispanic America, with an emphasis on the implications for the economic future of this country.

Equal Opportunity and the End of the "Lost Decade"

The past decade has been labeled the lost decade for American workers because of its record of zero net job growth, falling median incomes and declining net worth. With the slowest rate of economic output since the 1930s, never in modern history (or at least since the data has been collected) has the economy suffered so greatly over the course of a single decade. While these dismal facts are partially the result of bad timing—the decade both began and ended with recessions—they are equally the result of the two "jobless recoveries" that preceded the recessions. Based on data for 2008 and 2009, the statistics on unemployment, earnings, poverty and home ownership in this year's economic index capture some of the effects of the Great Recession.

Economics

The State of Black America 2010 appropriately focuses on the jobs crisis facing our nation. With a current jobs deficit of about 10-12 million jobs—the number needed to keep up with population growth and to recover the jobs lost during the recession—the increase in this year's unemployment rate index can be misleading. While an increase in the index represents a move toward greater employment "equality," it has been at the cost of higher rates of unemployment both for blacks (from 10.1% to 14.8%) and whites (from 5.2% to 8.5%). Still, the black-white unemployment rate index is only 57%. Although the Hispanic-white unemployment index is higher (70%), the 2009 average rate of unemployment for Hispanic workers was in the double digits as well (12.1%).

The small gain made last year in the gap between black and white real median household income was erased this year (from 65% to 62%) with the median black household earning $34,218 compared to $55,530 for the median white household. This decline in the index was brought about as the real median household income for whites increased faster than it did for blacks—up 7% and 1%, respectively. Real median household income for Hispanic households was $37,913.

The differences in unemployment and earnings are reflected in home ownership and poverty rates. Less than half of black and Hispanic families own a home—47.4% and 49.1%, respectively—compared to three-quarters of white families. Both blacks and Hispanics are also more than three times as likely as whites to live below the poverty line. Because wealth and poverty are often transferred intergenerationally, and we have yet to know the total fallout from the home foreclosure crisis, it is possible that these gaps will persist, or even worsen, from this generation to the next.

Health
Despite the tremendous effort to reform health care made by the Obama administration and some members of Congress in 2009, the real issues were soon overshadowed by a series of shouting matches and false PSAs. Unfortunately, at the end of the day, the fact remains that 10.8% of whites, 19.1% of blacks and 30.7% of Hispanics are without health insurance. In light of the disparities in health insurance coverage and the economic indicators discussed above, the disproportionate occurrence of the childhood obesity epidemic among minority populations is particularly troubling because of the myriad of costly health problems associated with being overweight. Among black children ages 6-11, 18.6% of boys and 24% of girls are overweight compared to 15.5% of white boys and 14.4% of white girls. For Hispanic children, the corresponding numbers are 27.5% of boys and 19.7% of girls.

Education
Around the world, education is seen as the single most effective engine of social and economic mobility. In America, for the population over age 25, whites are more than one and a half times as likely as blacks and two and a half times as likely as Hispanics to hold a bachelor's degree. Relative to the 2009 index, college enrollment data suggests that ground has been lost in terms closing this gap. Down from 90% the year before, the 2010 index shows that the black-white ratio of college enrollment rates for 18-24 year old high school completers is 84%. The corresponding

Hispanic-white ratio is 82%. In addition to the fact that college has grown increasingly unaffordable for low- to moderate-income families, another barrier to closing the overall attainment gap seems to be that the pool of high school completers for minority groups is smaller than that of whites. The high school dropout problem is especially serious within the Hispanic community with a dropout rate of 26.2% among 18-24 year olds compared to 13% of blacks and 10.8% of whites in the same age group.[2]

Social Justice
Finally, the economic future of our country will be directly influenced by the number of people we incarcerate relative to the number we educate and train for employment or entrepreneurship. Therefore, just as critical as closing the high school dropout gap is closing the incarceration gap. Though no new data was available for this year's index, Bureau of Justice Statistics data from 2008 indicate that blacks are six times more likely to be incarcerated than whites and Hispanics are three times more likely than whites.

Conclusion
Returning to the questions raised in the introduction of this report, the Equality Index presents some compelling evidence in favor of the need for a recovery and job creation plan that directly addresses the disparities facing large segments of the African American and Hispanic communities. First, in a nation where a growing segment of the population faces challenges to achieving equality in the areas of economics, education, health, social justice and civic engagement, it is vital to the economic future of this country to address these issues

head on. The future workforce of this country will undoubtedly reflect the increasingly diverse population of the country. If we are to maximize our potential as a nation and achieve optimal economic growth, we simply cannot afford to continue to undereducate, underemploy or underpay any persons. The urgency of this matter makes the mission of the National Urban League—civil rights and economic empowerment of historically underserved urban communities—just as important now as it was 100 years ago.

NOTES

[1] For negative outcomes like death rates or incarceration rates, the ratio is white-to-black so that the interpretation of the index (less than 100% suggests that blacks are doing worse relative to whites, and greater than 100% suggests that blacks are doing better than whites) is preserved.

[2] These dropout rates are known as status dropout rates. The status dropout rate measures the percentage of people within a certain age group who have not completed high school and are not currently enrolled.

INDEX

National Urban League 2010 Equality Index: Black-White
GLOBAL INSIGHT, INC.

Updated ▦ History Revised ▦ New Series Added in 2010

2010 EQUALITY INDEX OF BLACK AMERICA	Source	Year	Black	White	Index	Diff. ('10-'09)
Total Equality Weighted Index					71.8%	0.006

ECONOMICS (30%)

Median Income (0.25)

	Source	Year	Black	White	Index	Diff.
Median Household Income (Real), Dollars	Census	2008	34,218	55,530	62%	(0.03)
Median Male Earnings, Dollars	ACS	2008	36,355	50,767	72%	0.01
Median Female Earnings, Dollars	ACS	2008	31,658	37,358	85%	(0.01)

Poverty (0.15)

	Source	Year	Black	White	Index	Diff.
Population Living Below Poverty Line, %	Census	2008	24.7	8.6	35%	0.01
Population Living Below 50% of Poverty Line, %	Census	2008	11.4	3.7	32%	0.02
Population Living Below 125% of Poverty Line	Census	2008	31.6	12.1	38%	0.01
Population Living Below Poverty Line (Under 18), %	Census	2008	34.7	10.6	31%	0.01
Population Living Below Poverty Line (18-64), %	Census	2008	20.6	8.3	40%	0.01
Population Living Below Poverty Line (65 and Older), %	Census	2008	20	7.6	38%	0.06

Employment Issues (0.20)

	Source	Year	Black	White	Index	Diff.
Unemployment Rate, %	BLS	2009	14.8	8.5	57%	0.06
Unemployment Rate - Male, %	BLS	2009	17.5	9.4	54%	0.05
Unemployment Rate - Female, %	BLS	2009	12.4	7.3	59%	0.04
Unemployment Rate Persons 16 to 19, %	BLS	2009	39.5	21.8	55%	0.01
Percent not in Workforce - Ages 16 to 19, %	BLS	2009	72.8	59.4	82%	0.01
Percent not in Workforce- Ages 16 and Older, %	BLS	2009	37.6	34.2	91%	(0.02)
Labor Force Participation Rate, %	BLS	2009	62.4	65.8	95%	(0.01)
LFPR 16 to 19, %	BLS	2009	27.2	40.6	67%	(0.01)
LFPR 20 to 24, %	BLS	2009	66.0	75.1	88%	(0.01)
LFPR Over 25 - Less than High School Grad., %	BLS	2009	38.2	48.0	80%	(0.04)
LFPR Over 25 - High School Grad., No College, %	BLS	2009	64.6	61.7	105%	(0.01)
LFPR Over 25 - Some college, No Degree, %	BLS	2009	71.9	68.0	106%	(0.02)
LFPR Over 25 - Associate's Degree, %	BLS	2009	76.6	75.8	101%	(0.02)
LFPR Over 25 - Some College or Associate Degree, %	BLS	2009	73.4	70.8	104%	(0.02)
LFPR Over 25 - College Grad., %	BLS	2009	80.9	77.0	105%	
Employment to Pop. Ratio, %	BLS	2009	53.2	60.2	88%	(0.03)

Housing & Wealth (0.34)

	Source	Year	Black	White	Index	Diff.
Home Ownership Rate, %	Census	2008	47.4	75.0	63%	
Mortgage Application Denial Rate (Total), %	HMDA	2008	35.7	15.8	44%	(0.01)
Mortgage Application Denial Rate (Male), %	HMDA	2008	37.1	19.3	52%	0.02
Mortgage Application Denial Rate (Female), %	HMDA	2008	36.6	18.7	51%	
Mortgage Application Denial Rate (Joint), %	HMDA	2008	31.2	11.6	37%	(0.03)
Home Improvement Loans Denials (Total), %	HMDA	2008	60.8	35.8	59%	(0.01)
Home Improvement Loans Denials (Male), %	HMDA	2008	61.5	40.8	66%	
Home Improvement Loans Denials (Female), %	HMDA	2008	62.1	40.7	66%	
Home Improvement Loans Denials (Joint), %	HMDA	2008	56.7	29.6	52%	(0.03)

2010 EQUALITY INDEX OF BLACK AMERICA	Source	Year	Black	White	Index	Diff. ('10-'09)
Percent of High-Priced Loans (More than 3% Above Treasury)	HMDA	2008	17.2	6.5	38%	0.07
Median Home Value, Dollars	Census	2000	80,600	123,400	65%	
Median Wealth, 2005 Dollars	PSID	2007	9,500	116,500	8%	(0.01)
Equity in Home, Dollars	Census	2002	40,000	79,200	51%	
Percent Investing in 401K, %	EBRI	2005	27.0	36.8	73%	
Percent Investing in IRA, %	EBRI	2005	9.9	27.7	36%	
U.S. Firms by Race (% Compared to Employment Share)	Census	2002	0.51	0.95	54%	
Digital Divide (0.05)						
Households with Computer at Home, %	Census	2005	44.8	64.6	69%	0.02
Households with the Internet, %	Census	2007	45.3	66.9	68%	
Adult Users with Broadband Access, %	Pew Internet & American Life Project	2009	46.0	65.0	71%	(0.05)
Transportation (0.01)						
Car Ownership, %	Census	2002	67.1	88.4	76%	
Means of Transportation to Work: Drive Alone, %	ACS	2008	70.6	79.0	89%	
Means of Transportation to Work: Public Transportation, %	ACS	2008	11.8	2.9	25%	
Economic Weighted Index					57.4%	0.001

HEALTH (25%)						
Death Rates & Life Expectancy (0.45)						
Life Expectancy at Birth	CDC	2006	73.2	78.2	94%	
Male	CDC	2006	69.7	75.7	92%	
Female	CDC	2006	76.5	80.6	95%	
Life Expectancy at 65 (Additional Expected Years)	CDC	2006	17.1	18.6	92%	0.01
Male at 65	CDC	2006	15.1	17.1	88%	0.01
Female at 65	CDC	2006	18.6	19.8	94%	0.01
Age-Adjusted Death Rates (per 100,000)- All Causes	CDC	2006	1,001.4	777.0	78%	(0.01)
Age-Adjusted Death Rates (per 100,000)- Male	CDC	2006	1,241.0	922.8	74%	(0.01)
Age-Adjusted Death Rates (per 100,000)- Female	CDC	2006	828.4	660.0	80%	
Age-Adjusted Death Rates (per 100,000)- Heart Disease	CDC	2006	262.3	200.3	76%	(0.01)
Ischemic Heart Disease	CDC	2006	164.1	136.0	83%	(0.02)
Age-Adjusted Death Rates (per 100,000)- Stroke (Cerebrovascular)	CDC	2006	62.8	41.9	67%	(0.02)
Age-Adjusted Death Rates (per 100,000)- Cancer	CDC	2006	221.7	184.6	83%	(0.01)
Trachea, Bronchus, and Lung	CDC	2006	57.9	54.7	94%	(0.01)
Colon, Rectum, and Anus	CDC	2006	24.7	17.0	69%	(0.01)
Prostate (Male)	CDC	2006	18.5	21.9	118%	0.76
Breast (Female)	CDC	2006	19.0	23.5	124%	0.51
Age-Adjusted Death Rates (per 100,000)- Chronic Lower Respiratory	CDC	2006	28.6	44.4	155%	0.01
Age-Adjusted Death Rates (per 100,000)-Influenza and Pneumonia	CDC	2006	19.9	17.8	89%	(0.04)
Age-Adjusted Death Rates (per 100,000)-Chronic Liver Disease & Cirrhosis	CDC	2006	7.1	8.6	121%	0.08

2010 EQUALITY INDEX OF BLACK AMERICA	Source	Year	Black	White	Index	Diff. ('10-'09)
Age-Adjusted Death Rates (per 100,000)- Diabetes	CDC	2006	45.9	20.4	44%	(0.01)
Age-Adjusted Death Rates (per 100,000)- HIV	CDC	2006	19.1	1.7	9%	
Unintentional Injuries	CDC	2006	39.2	42.1	107%	0.01
Motor Vehicle-Related Injuries	CDC	2006	15.9	15.3	96%	(0.11)
Age-Adjusted Death Rates (per 100,000)- Suicide	CDC	2006	5.2	13.2	254%	0.06
Age-Adjusted Death Rates (per 100,000)- Suicide Males	CDC	2006	9.6	21.4	223%	(0.08)
Age-Adjusted Death Rates (per 100,000)- Suicide Males Ages 15-24	CDC	2006	10.6	18.5	175%	0.15
Age-Adjusted Death Rates (per 100,000)- Suicide Females	CDC	2006	1.4	5.6	400%	1.21
Age-Adjusted Death Rates (per 100,000)- Suicide Females Ages 15-24	CDC	2006	1.8	3.5	194%	(0.35)
Age-Adjusted Death Rates (per 100,000)- Homicide	CDC	2006	22.4	2.7	12%	(0.01)
Age-Adjusted Death Rates (per 100,000)- Homicide Male	CDC	2006	39.2	3.6	9%	
Age-Adjusted Death Rates (per 100,000)- Homicide Males Ages 15-24	CDC	2006	88.2	4.7	5%	
Age-Adjusted Death Rates (per 100,000)- Homicide Female	CDC	2006	6.7	1.8	27%	(0.03)
Age-Adjusted Death Rates (per 100,000)- Homicide Females Ages 15-24	CDC	2006	9.5	2.0	21%	(0.02)
Age-Adjusted Death Rates (per 100,000) by Age Cohort: >1 Male	CDC	2006	1,407.1	621.9	44%	0.01
Age-Adjusted Death Rates (per 100,000) by Age Cohort: 1-4 Male	CDC	2006	47.1	26.7	57%	(0.07)
Age-Adjusted Death Rates (per 100,000) by Age Cohort: 5-14 Male	CDC	2006	24.8	16.2	65%	0.01
Age-Adjusted Death Rates (per 100,000) by Age Cohort: 15-24 Male	CDC	2006	171.3	107.6	63%	0.01
Age-Adjusted Death Rates (per 100,000) by Age Cohort: 25-34 Male	CDC	2006	254.2	141.1	56%	0.03
Age-Adjusted Death Rates (per 100,000) by Age Cohort: 35-44 Male	CDC	2006	392.3	233.1	59%	
Age-Adjusted Death Rates (per 100,000) by Age Cohort: 45-54 Male	CDC	2006	921.9	515.1	56%	0.01
Age-Adjusted Death Rates (per 100,000) by Age Cohort: 55-64 Male	CDC	2006	1,891.8	1,064.0	56%	0.01
Age-Adjusted Death Rates (per 100,000) by Age Cohort: 65-74 Male	CDC	2006	3,669.2	2,490.3	68%	(0.01)
Age-Adjusted Death Rates (per 100,000) by Age Cohort: 75-84 Male	CDC	2006	7,393.2	6278.3	85%	0.01
Age-Adjusted Death Rates (per 100,000) by Age Cohort: 85+ Male	CDC	2006	13,206.0	14,841.1	112%	0.01
Age-Adjusted Death Rates (per 100,000) by Age Cohort: >1 Female	CDC	2006	1,194.6	503.7	42%	
Age-Adjusted Death Rates (per 100,000) by Age Cohort: 1-4 Female	CDC	2006	39.4	23.2	59%	(0.02)
Age-Adjusted Death Rates (per 100,000) by Age Cohort: 5-14 Female	CDC	2006	17.4	11.8	68%	0.01
Age-Adjusted Death Rates (per 100,000) by Age Cohort: 15-24 Female	CDC	2006	51.3	42.9	84%	0.01
Age-Adjusted Death Rates (per 100,000) by Age Cohort: 25-34 Female	CDC	2006	106.6	62.5	59%	0.02
Age-Adjusted Death Rates (per 100,000) by Age Cohort: 35-44 Female	CDC	2006	245.0	136.3	56%	0.01
Age-Adjusted Death Rates (per 100,000) by Age Cohort: 45-54 Female	CDC	2006	548.1	299.8	55%	0.02
Age-Adjusted Death Rates (per 100,000) by Age Cohort: 55-64 Female	CDC	2006	1,076.3	668.0	62%	0.01
Age-Adjusted Death Rates (per 100,000) by Age Cohort: 65-74 Female	CDC	2006	2,239.7	1,677.4	75%	0.01
Age-Adjusted Death Rates (per 100,000) by Age Cohort: 75-84 Female	CDC	2006	5,028.9	4,460.7	89%	0.02
Age-Adjusted Death Rates (per 100,000) by Age Cohort: 85+ Female	CDC	2006	12,196.7	13,150.7	108%	0.01
Physical Condition (0.10)						
Overweight: 18+ Years, % of Population	CDC	2008	35.2	36.3	103%	
Overweight - Men 20 Years and Over, % of Population	CDC	2003-2006	36.0	39.4	109%	
Overweight - Women 20 Years and Over, % of Population	CDC	2003-2006	26.4	26.3	100%	
Obese, % of Population	CDC	2008	36.8	25.4	69%	(0.01)

Updated ▨ History Revised ▨ New Series Added in 2010

2010 EQUALITY INDEX OF BLACK AMERICA	Source	Year	Black	White	Index	Diff. ('10-'09)
Obese - Men 20 Years and Over, % of Population	CDC	2003-2006	35.3	32.2	91%	
Obese - Women 20 Years and Over, % of Population	CDC	2003-2006	53.0	31.7	60%	
Diabetes: Physician Diagnosed in Ages 20+, % of Population	CDC	2003-2006	13.2	6.4	48%	(0.04)
AIDS Cases per 100,000 Males Ages 13+	CDC	2007	81.3	10.6	13%	
AIDS Cases per 100,000 Females Ages 13+	CDC	2007	39.8	1.8	5%	
Substance Abuse (0.10)						
Binge Alcohol (5 Drinks in 1 day, 1x a year) Ages 18+, % of Population	CDC	2007	11.8	24.4	207%	0.06
Use of Illicit Drugs in the Past Month Ages 12+, % of Population	CDC	2007	9.5	8.2	86%	0.03
Tobacco: Both Cigarette & Cigar Ages 12+, % of Population	CDC	2007	26.8	30.7	115%	0.05
Mental Health (0.02)						
Students Who Consider Suicide: Male, %	CDC	2007	8.5	10.2	120%	(0.57)
Students Who Carry Out Intent and Require Medical Attention: Male, %	CDC	2007	2.5	0.9	36%	(0.71)
Students That Act on Suicidal Feeling: Male, %	CDC	2007	5.5	3.4	62%	(0.38)
Students Who Consider Suicide: Female, %	CDC	2007	18.0	17.8	99%	(0.27)
Students Who Carry Out Intent and Require Medical Attention: Female, %	CDC	2007	2.1	2.1	100%	(0.04)
Students That Act on Suicidal Feeling: Female, %	CDC	2007	9.9	7.7	78%	(0.17)
Access to Care (0.05)						
Private Insurance Payment for Health Care: Under 65 years old, % of Distribution	CDC	2006	41.3	58.3	71%	0.04
People Without Health Insurance, % of Population	Census	2008	19.1	10.8	57%	0.03
People 18 to 64 Without a Usual Source of Health Insurance, % of Adults	Census	2008	25.3	14.6	57%	0.03
People in Poverty Without a Usual Source of Health Insurance, % of Adults	Census	2008	38.3	38.5	101%	0.08
Population Under 65 Covered by Medicaid, % of Population	CDC	2007	27.3	8.5	31%	(0.05)
Elderly Health Care (0.03)						
Population Over 65 Covered by Medicaid, % of Population	CDC	2007	18.8	5.7	30%	0.04
Medicare Expenditures per Beneficiary, Dollars	CDC	2006	17,865	15,587	87%	0.15
Pregnancy Issues (0.04)						
Prenatal Care Begins in 1st Trimester	CDC	2006	76.1	88.1	86%	0.01
Prenatal Rare Begins in 3rd Trimester	CDC	2006	5.7	2.3	40%	0.04
Percent of Births to Mothers 18 and Under	CDC	2006	6.3	2.0	32%	
Percent of Live Births to Unmarried Mothers	CDC	2006	70.7	26.6	38%	0.01
Infant Mortality Rates Among Mothers 20 years of Age and Over, by Education						
Less than 12 years Education	CDC	2005	13.8	6.5	47%	
12 Years Education	CDC	2005	13.8	6.6	48%	
13 Years or More Education	CDC	2005	11.1	4.2	38%	
Mothers Who Smoked Cigarettes During Pregnancy, %	CDC	2006	7.9	13.3	168%	0.07
Low Birth Weight, % of Live Births	CDC	2006	14.0	7.3	52%	
Very Low Birth Weight, % of Live Births	CDC	2006	3.2	1.2	38%	
Reproduction Issues (0.01)						
Abortions, per 100 Live Births	CDC	2005	46.7	15.8	34%	
Women Using Contraception, % of Population	CDC	2002	57.6	64.6	89%	

Updated ▓ History Revised ▓ New Series Added in 2010

2010 EQUALITY INDEX OF BLACK AMERICA	Source	Year	Black	White	Index	Diff.('10-'09)
Delivery Issues (0.10)						
All Infant Deaths: Neonatal and Post, per 1000 Live Births	CDC	2005	13.6	5.8	43%	
Neonatal Deaths, per 1000 live Births	CDC	2005	9.1	3.7	41%	
PostNeonatal Deaths, per 1000 Live Births	CDC	2005	4.5	2.1	47%	
Maternal Mortality, per 100,000 Live Births	CDC	2006	28.7	8.0	28%	(0.02)
Children's Health (0.10)						
Babies Breastfed, %	CDC	2006	56.5	73.8	77%	0.11
Children Without a Health Care Visit in Past 12 Months (p to 6 years old), %	CDC	2006-2007	4.7	6.1	130%	0.16
Vaccinations of Children Below Poverty: Combined Vacc. Series 4:3:1:3, % of Children 19-35 Months	CDC	2007	74.0	70.0	106%	0.01
Uninsured Children, %	Census	2008	10.7	6.7	63%	0.03
Overweight Boys 6-11 Years Old, % of Population	CDC	2003-2006	18.6	15.5	83%	(0.15)
Overweight Girls 6-11 Years Old, % of Population	CDC	2003-2006	24.0	14.4	60%	(0.03)
AIDS Cases per 100,000 All Children Under 13	CDC	2007	21.0	5.0	24%	0.10
Health Weighted Index					**77.0%**	**0.001**

EDUCATION (25%)						
Quality (.25)						
Teacher Quality (.10)						
Middle Grades - Teacher Lacking at Least a College Minor in Subject Taught (High vs. Low Minority Schools), %	ET	2000	49.0	40.0	85%	
HS - Teacher Lacking an Undergraduate Major in Subject Taught (High vs. Low Minority Schools), %	ET	2000	28.0	21.0	91%	
Per Student Funding (High vs. Low Poverty Districts), Dollars	ET	2004	5,937	7,244	82%	
Teachers with <3 Years Experience (High vs. Low Minority Schools) , %	NCES	2000	21.0	10.0	48%	
Distribution of Underprepared Teachers (High vs. Low Minority Schools), % (California Only)	SRI	2007-2008	7.0	2.0	29%	(0.09)
Course Quality (0.15)						
College Completion, % of All Entrants	ET	1999	45.0	73.0	62%	
College Completion, % of Entrants with Strong HS Curriculum (Algebra II plus Other Courses)	ET	1999	75.0	86.0	87%	
HS Students: Enrolled in Chemistry, %	NCES	2005	63.6	67.1	95%	
HS Students: Enrolled in Algebra 2, %	NCES	2005	69.2	71.2	97%	
Students Taking: Precalculus, %	CB	2009	36.0	55.0	65%	0.02
Students Taking: Calculus, %	CB	2009	14.0	30.0	47%	(0.02)
Students Taking: Physics, %	CB	2009	44.0	54.0	81%	0.03
Students Taking: English Honors Course, %	CB	2009	31.0	43.0	72%	(0.04)
Attainment (0.30)						
Graduation Rates, 2-year Institutions, %	NCES	2002	27.2	33.8	80%	
Graduation Rates, 4-year Institutions, %	NCES	1999	40.4	58.9	69%	
NCAA Div. I College Freshmen Graduating Within 6 years, %	NCAA	2001-2002	45.0	65.0	69%	

2010 EQUALITY INDEX OF BLACK AMERICA	Source	Year	Black	White	Index	Diff. ('10-'09)
Degrees Earned: Associate, % of Population Aged 18-24 Years	NCES	2007	2.1	2.7	76%	
Degrees Earned: Bachelor's, % of Population Aged 18-29 Years	NCES	2007	2.0	3.6	55%	
Degrees Earned: Master's, % of Population Aged 18-34 Years	NCES	2007	0.6	0.9	66%	0.02
Educational Attainment: At Least High School (25 Years. and Over), % of Population	Census	2008	83.0	91.5	91%	
Educational Attainment: At Least Bachelor's (25 Years and Over), % of Population	Census	2008	19.6	32.6	60%	0.02
Degree Holders, % Distribution, by Field						
Agriculture/Forestry	NCES	2001	0.7	1.2	56%	
Art/Architecture	NCES	2001	3.3	2.9	114%	
Business/Management	NCES	2001	19.5	18.1	108%	
Communications	NCES	2001	3.2	2.4	135%	
Computer and Information Sciences	NCES	2001	3.9	2.2	177%	
Education	NCES	2001	15.3	15.3	100%	
Engineering	NCES	2001	3.6	7.7	47%	
English/Literature	NCES	2001	2.6	3.3	80%	
Foreign Languages	NCES	2001	0.8	0.9	96%	
Health Sciences	NCES	2001	5.4	4.5	120%	
Liberal arts/Humanities	NCES	2001	4.6	6.1	75%	
Mathematics/Statistics	NCES	2001	2.4	1.4	169%	
Natural Sciences	NCES	2001	6.0	5.6	106%	
Philosophy/Religion/Theology	NCES	2001	0.9	1.3	70%	
Pre-Professional	NCES	2001	1.6	1.1	146%	
Psychology	NCES	2001	4.9	3.9	126%	
Social Sciences/History	NCES	2001	8.1	4.9	165%	
Other Fields	NCES	2001	13.1	17.2	76%	
Scores (.25)						
Preschool 10% of Total Scores (0.015)						
Children's School Readiness Skills (Ages 3-5), % With 3 or 4 Skills* *Recognizes all letters, counts to 20 or higher, writes name, reads or pretends to read	NCES	2005	44.1	46.8	94%	
Elementary 40% of Total Scores (0.06)						
Average Scale Score in U.S. History, 8th Graders	NCES	2006	244	273	89%	
Average Scale Score in U.S. History, 4th Graders	NCES	2006	191	223	86%	
Average Scale Score in Math, 8th Graders	NCES	2007	260	291	89%	0.01
Average Scale Score in Math, 4th Graders	NCES	2007	222	248	90%	
Average Scale Score in Reading, 8th Graders	NCES	2007	245	272	90%	
Average Scale Score in Reading, 4th Graders	NCES	2007	203	231	88%	0.01
Average Scale Score in Science, 8th Graders	NCES	2005	124	160	78%	
Average Scale Score in Science, 4th Graders	NCES	2005	129	162	80%	
Writing Proficiency at or Above Basic, 8th Graders, % of Students	NCES	2007	81	93	87%	0.05
Writing Proficiency at or Above Basic, 4th Graders, % of Students	NCES	2002	77	90	85%	
High School 50% of Total Scores (0.075)						

Updated ▓ History Revised ▬ New Series Added in 2010

2010 EQUALITY INDEX OF BLACK AMERICA	Source	Year	Black	White	Index	Diff. ('10-'09)
Writing Proficiency at or Above Basic, 12th Graders, % of Students	NCES	2007	69	86	80%	0.05
Average Scale Score in Science, 12th Graders	NCES	2005	120	156	77%	
Average Scale Score in U.S. History, 12th Graders	NCES	2006	270	297	91%	
Average Scale Score in Reading, 12th Graders	NCES	2005	267	293	91%	
High School GPA's for Those Taking the SAT	CB	2008	3.0	3.4	89%	0.01
SAT Reasoning Test - Mean Scores	CB	2009	1,276	1,581	81%	
Mathematics, Joint	CB	2009	426	536	79%	
Mathematics, Male	CB	2009	435	555	78%	
Mathematics, Female	CB	2009	420	520	81%	
Critical Reading, Joint	CB	2009	429	528	81%	
Critical Reading, Male	CB	2009	426	530	80%	
Critical Reading, Female	CB	2009	431	526	82%	
Writing, Joint	CB	2009	421	517	81%	
Writing, Male	CB	2009	410	509	81%	
Writing, Female	CB	2009	429	524	82%	
ACT - Average Composite Score	ACT	2009	13.0	22.2	59%	(0.18)
Enrollment (0.10)						
School Enrollment: Ages 3-34, % of Population	Census	2008	57.8	56.7	102%	
Preprimary School Enrollment	Census	2008	63.6	66.5	96%	(0.02)
3 and 4 Years Old	Census	2008	54.6	56.0	98%	(0.04)
5 and 6 Years Old	Census	2008	93.1	94.9	98%	0.01
7 to 13 Years Old	Census	2008	98.9	98.9	100%	0.01
14 and 15 Years Old	Census	2008	97.9	98.8	99%	
16 and 17 Years Old	Census	2008	94.2	95.9	98%	0.01
18 and 19 Years Old	Census	2008	59.2	70.0	85%	(0.11)
20 and 21 Years Old	Census	2008	40.3	55.8	72%	(0.02)
22 to 24 Years Old	Census	2008	24.9	30.3	82%	(0.17)
25 to 29 Years Old	Census	2008	14.7	13.3	111%	0.16
30 to 34 Years Old	Census	2008	11.5	6.9	167%	0.50
35 Years Old and Over	Census	2008	2.8	1.8	159%	(0.23)
College Enrollment (Graduate or Undergraduate): Ages 14 and Over, % of Population	Census	2008	6.9	6.5	106%	(0.02)
14 to 17 Years Old	Census	2008	1.4	1.2	113%	0.14
18 to 19 Years Old	Census	2008	35.9	55.0	65%	(0.09)
20 to 21 Years Old	Census	2008	36.8	54.9	67%	0.01
22 to 24 Years Old	Census	2008	24.4	30.1	81%	(0.19)
25 to 29 Years Old	Census	2008	13.3	13.0	102%	0.12
30 to 34 Years Old	Census	2008	11.0	6.9	159%	0.47
35 Years Old and Over	Census	2008	2.6	1.7	157%	(0.20)
College Enrollment Rate as a Percent of All 18- to 24-year-old High School Completers, %	NCES	2007	40.1	47.8	84%	(0.07)
Adult Education Participation, % of Adult Population	NCES	2004-05	46.0	46.0	100%	

2010 EQUALITY INDEX OF BLACK AMERICA	Source	Year	Black	White	Index	Diff. ('10-'09)
Student Status & Risk Factors (.10)						
High School Dropouts: Status Dropouts, % (not Completed HS and not Enrolled, Regardless of When Dropped)	Census	2006	13.0	10.8	83%	(0.05)
Children in Poverty, %	Census	2008	34.7	10.6	31%	0.02
Children in All Families Below Poverty Level, %	Census	2008	34.4	10.0	29%	
Children in Families Below Poverty Level (Female Householder, no Spouse Present), %	Census	2008	51.9	31.6	61%	(0.05)
Children with no Parent in the Labor Force, %	USDC	2000	20.3	5.5	27%	
Children (under 18) with a Disability, %	Census	2008	4.9	4.0	81%	
Public School Students (K-12): Repeated Grade, %	NCES	2003	17.1	8.2	48%	
Public School Students (K-12): Suspended, %	NCES	2003	19.6	8.8	45%	
Public School Students (K-12): Expelled, %	NCES	2003	5.0	1.4	28%	
Center-Based Child Care of Preschool Children, %	NCES	2005	66.5	59.1	89%	
Parental Care Only of Preschool Children, %	NCES	2005	19.5	24.1	81%	
Teacher Stability: Remained in Public School, High vs. Low Minority Schools, %	NCES	2005	79.7	85.9	93%	
Teacher Stability: Remained in Private School, High vs. Low Minority Schools, %	NCES	2005	72.7	82.8	88%	
Zero Days Missed in School Year, % of 10th Graders	NCES	2002	16.5	13.0	127%	
3+ Days Late to School, % of 10th Graders	NCES	2002	46.1	31.5	68%	
Never Cut Classes, % of 10th Graders	NCES	2002	64.6	72.9	89%	
Home Literacy Activities (Age 3 to 5)						
Read to Three or More Times a Week	NCES	2005	78.5	91.9	85%	
Told a Story at Least Once a Month	NCES	2005	54.3	53.3	102%	
Taught Words or Numbers Three or More Times a Week	NCES	2005	80.6	75.7	107%	
Visited a Library at Least Once in Last Month	NCES	2005	43.9	44.9	98%	
Education Weighted Index					77.6%	0.006

SOCIAL JUSTICE (10%)						
Equality Before the Law (0.70)						
Stopped While Driving, %	BJS	2005	8.1	8.9	110%	
Speeding	BJS	2002	50.0	57.0	114%	
Vehicle Defect	BJS	2002	10.3	8.7	84%	
Roadside Check for Drinking Drivers	BJS	2002	1.1	1.3	118%	
Record Check	BJS	2002	17.4	11.3	65%	
Seatbelt Violation	BJS	2002	3.5	4.4	126%	
Illegal Turn/Lane Change	BJS	2002	5.1	4.5	88%	
Stop Sign/Light Violation	BJS	2002	5.9	6.5	110%	
Other	BJS	2002	3.7	4.0	108%	
Mean Incarceration Sentence (in Average Months)	BJS	2004	40	37	93%	
Average Sentence for Incarceration (All Offenses) - Male, Months	BJS	2004	43	39	91%	

2010 EQUALITY INDEX OF BLACK AMERICA	Source	Year	Black	White	Index	Diff. ('10-'09)
Average Sentence for Murder - Male, Months	BJS	2004	256	232	91%	
Average Sentence for Sexual Assault	BJS	2004	104	110	106%	
Average Sentence for Robbery	BJS	2004	101	88	87%	
Average Sentence for Aggravated Assault	BJS	2004	51	42	82%	
Average Sentence for Other Violent	BJS	2004	47	43	91%	
Average Sentence for Burglary	BJS	2004	47	44	94%	
Average Sentence for Larceny	BJS	2004	23	21	91%	
Average Sentence for Fraud	BJS	2004	25	27	108%	
Average Sentence for Drug Possession	BJS	2004	23	22	96%	
Average Sentence for Drug Trafficking	BJS	2004	38	41	108%	
Average Sentence for Weapon Offenses	BJS	2004	34	32	94%	
Average Sentence for Other Offenses	BJS	2004	25	25	100%	
Average Sentence for Incarceration (All Offenses) - Female, Months	BJS	2004	23	24	104%	
Average Sentence for Murder	BJS	2004	231	152	66%	
Average Sentence for Sexual Assault	BJS	2004	55	88	160%	
Average Sentence for Robbery	BJS	2004	80	55	69%	
Average Sentence for Aggravated Assault	BJS	2004	31	31	100%	
Average Sentence for Other Violent	BJS	2004	31	41	132%	
Average Sentence for Burglary	BJS	2004	22	27	123%	
Average Sentence for Larceny	BJS	2004	17	17	100%	
Average Sentence for Fraud	BJS	2004	21	21	100%	
Average Sentence for Drug Possession	BJS	2004	15	16	107%	
Average Sentence for Drug Trafficking	BJS	2004	25	28	112%	
Average Sentence for Weapon Offenses	BJS	2004	20	26	130%	
Average Sentence for Other Offenses	BJS	2004	17	20	118%	
Convicted Felons Sentenced to Probation, All Offenses, %	BJS	2004	26	30	87%	
Probation Sentence for Murder, %	BJS	2004	5	6	83%	
Probation Sentence for Sexual Assault, %	BJS	2004	17	18	94%	
Probation Sentence for Robbery, %	BJS	2004	11	13	85%	
Probation Sentence for Burglary, %	BJS	2004	22	25	88%	
Probation Sentence for Fraud, %	BJS	2004	40	38	105%	
Probation Sentence for Drug Offenses, %	BJS	2004	26	34	76%	
Probation Sentence for Weapon Offenses, %	BJS	2004	29	25	116%	
Incarceration Rate: Prisoners per 100,000	BJS	2008	2,126	334	16%	
Incarceration Rate: Prisoners per 100,000 People - Male	BJS	2008	3,161	487	15%	
Incarceration Rate: Prisoners per 100,000 People - Female	BJS	2008	149	50	34%	
Prisoners as a % of Arrests	FBI, BJS	2007	23.5	8.3	35%	
Victimization & Mental Anguish (0.30)						
Homicide Rate per 100,000	BJS	2005	20.6	3.3	16%	
Homicide Rate per 100,000: Firearm	NACJD	2007	14.9	1.7	12%	(0.03)
Homicide Rate per 100,000: Stabbings	NACJD	2007	1.8	0.4	23%	(0.02)

| | Updated | History Revised | New Series Added in 2010 |

2010 EQUALITY INDEX OF BLACK AMERICA	Source	Year	Black	White	Index	Diff. ('10-'09)
Homicide Rate per 100,000: Personal Weapons	NACJD	2007	0.6	0.2	38%	(1.59)
Homicide Rate per 100,000 - Male	CDC	2006	40.6	3.6	9%	
Homicide Rate per 100,000 - Female	CDC	2006	6.6	1.8	27%	(0.02)
Murder Victims, Rate per 100,000	USDJ	2008	17.4	2.8	16%	0.01
Hate Crimes Victims, Rate per 100,000	USDJ	2007	8.8	0.4	4%	(0.02)
Victims of Violent Crimes, Rate per 100,000	BJS	2008	25.9	18.1	70%	(0.01)
Delinquency Cases, Year of Disposition, Rate per 100,000	NCJJ	2005	3,059.3	1,342.1	44%	
Prisoners Under Sentence of Death, Rate per 100,000	BJS	2007	5.1	1.2	23%	(0.01)
High School Students Carrying Weapons on School Property	CDC	2007	6.0	5.3	88%	
High School Students Carrying Weapons Anywhere	CDC	2007	17.2	18.2	106%	
Firearm-Related Death Rates per 100,000: Males, All Ages	CDC	2006	41.8	15.7	37%	(0.02)
Ages 1-14	CDC	2006	2.4	0.7	29%	(0.10)
Ages 15-24	CDC	2006	95.5	13.9	15%	(0.01)
Ages 25-44	CDC	2006	66.7	17.1	26%	(0.01)
Ages 25-34	CDC	2006	93.8	16.3	17%	(0.01)
Ages 35-44	CDC	2006	39.5	17.8	45%	0.01
Ages 45-64	CDC	2006	19.7	19.5	99%	(0.11)
Age 65 and Older	CDC	2006	13.4	27.3	203%	(0.03)
Firearm-Related Death Rates per 100,000: Females, All Ages	CDC	2006	4.3	2.8	67%	(0.06)
Ages 1-14	CDC	2006	0.9	0.3	33%	
Ages 15-24	CDC	2006	7.9	2.2	28%	(0.04)
Ages 25-44	CDC	2006	7.3	3.8	52%	(0.11)
Ages 25-34	CDC	2006	8.8	3.1	35%	
Ages 35-44	CDC	2006	5.8	4.4	75%	
Ages 45-64	CDC	2006	2.7	4.2	158%	0.17
Age 65 and Older	CDC	2006	1.0	2.2	208%	0.35
Social Justice Weighted Index					57.1%	(0.001)

CIVIC ENGAGEMENT (10%)						
Democratic Process (0.4)						
Registered Voters, % of Citizen Population	Census	2008	69.7	73.5	95%	0.09
Actually Voted, % of Citizen Population	Census	2008	64.7	66.1	98%	0.18
Community Participation (0.3)						
Percent of Population Volunteering for Military Reserves, %	USDD	2007	0.9	1.0	90%	(0.05)
Volunteerism, %	BLS	2008	19.1	27.9	68%	0.03
Civic and Political	BLS	2008	4.3	5.6	77%	
Educational or Youth Service	BLS	2008	22.9	26.1	88%	(0.05)
Environmental or Animal Care	BLS	2008	0.3	2.2	14%	(0.15)
Hospital or Other Health	BLS	2008	6.3	8.5	74%	0.11
Public Safety	BLS	2008	0.2	1.4	14%	0.01

Updated   History Revised   New Series Added in 2010

2010 EQUALITY INDEX OF BLACK AMERICA	Source	Year	Black	White	Index	Diff. ('10-'09)
Religious	BLS	2008	46.5	33.9	137%	(0.02)
Social or Community Service	BLS	2008	12.7	13.8	92%	0.03
Unpaid Volunteering of Young Adults	NCES	2000	40.9	32.2	127%	
Collective Bargaining (0.2)						
Members of Unions, % of Employed	BLS	2008	14.5	12.2	119%	(0.02)
Represented by Unions, % of Employed	BLS	2008	15.8	13.5	117%	(0.05)
Governmental Employment (0.1)						
Federal Executive Branch (Nonpostal) Employment, % of Adult Population	OPM	2006	1.2	0.8	146%	
State and Local Government Employment, %	EEOC	2005	4.2	2.6	162%	(0.05)
Civic Engagement Weighted Index					102.2%	0.047

INDEX

National Urban League 2010 Equality Index: Hispanic-White
GLOBAL INSIGHT, INC.

Different Source/Year for Hispanic-White Index than Black-White Index

2010 EQUALITY INDEX OF HISPANIC AMERICA	Source	Year	Hispanic	White	Index	Comparable Black-White Index
Total Equality Weighted Index					75.5%	73.0%

ECONOMICS (30%)

Median Income (0.25)

Median Household Income (Real), Dollars	Census	2008	37,913	55,530	68%	62%
Median Male Earnings, Dollars	ACS	2008	30,842	50,767	61%	72%
Median Female Earnings, Dollars	ACS	2008	26,593	37,358	71%	85%

Poverty (0.15)

Population Living Below Poverty Line, %	Census	2008	23.2	8.6	37%	35%
Population Living Below 50% of Poverty Line, %	Census	2008	9.1	3.7	41%	32%
Population Living Below 125% of Poverty Line	Census	2008	31.4	12.1	39%	38%
Population Living Below Poverty Line (Under 18), %	Census	2008	30.6	10.6	35%	31%
Population Living Below Poverty Line (18-64), %	Census	2008	19.3	8.3	43%	40%
Population Living Below Poverty Line (65 and Older), %	Census	2008	19.3	7.6	39%	38%

Employment Issues (0.20)

Unemployment Rate, %	BLS	2009	12.1	8.5	70%	57%
Unemployment Rate - Male, %	BLS	2009	12.5	9.4	75%	54%
Unemployment Rate - Female, %	BLS	2009	11.5	7.3	63%	59%
Unemployment Rate Persons 16-19, %	BLS	2009	27.8	21.8	78%	55%
Percent Not in Workforce - Ages 16 to 19, %	BLS	2009	66.0	59.4	90%	82%
Percent Not in Workforce- Ages 16 and Older, %	BLS	2009	32.0	34.2	107%	91%
Labor Force Participation Rate, %	BLS	2009	68.0	65.8	103%	95%
LFPR 16 to 19, %	BLS	2009	34.0	40.6	84%	67%
LFPR 20 to 24, %	BLS	2009	73.1	75.1	97%	88%
LFPR Over 25 - Less than High School Grad., %	BLS	2009	62.1	48.0	129%	80%
LFPR Over 25 - High School Grad., No College, %	BLS	2009	73.1	61.7	118%	105%
LFPR Over 25 - Some College, No Degree, %	BLS	2009	78.0	68.0	115%	106%
LFPR Over 25 - Associate's Degree, %	BLS	2009	80.7	75.8	106%	101%
LFPR Over 25 - Some College or Associate Degree, %	BLS	2009	78.9	70.8	111%	104%
LFPR Over 25 - College Grad., %	BLS	2009	81.7	77.0	106%	105%
Employment to Pop. Ratio, %	BLS	2009	59.7	60.2	99%	88%

Housing & Wealth (0.34)

Home Ownership Rate, %	Census	2008	49.1	75.0	65%	63%
Mortgage Application Denial Rate (Total), %	HMDA	2008	29.2	15.8	54%	44%
Mortgage Application Denial Rate (Male), %	HMDA	2008	30.7	19.3	63%	52%
Mortgage Application Denial Rate (Female), %	HMDA	2008	30.7	18.7	61%	51%
Mortgage Application Denial Rate (Joint), %	HMDA	2008	25.1	11.6	46%	37%
Home Improvement Loans Denials (Total), %	HMDA	2008	54.7	35.8	66%	59%
Home Improvement Loans Denials (Male), %	HMDA	2008	56.8	40.8	72%	66%
Home Improvement Loans Denials (Female), %	HMDA	2008	57.9	40.7	70%	66%
Home Improvement Loans Denials (Joint), %	HMDA	2008	48.8	29.6	61%	52%

2010 EQUALITY INDEX OF HISPANIC AMERICA	Source	Year	Hispanic	White	Index	Comparable Black-White Index
Percent of High-Priced Loans (More than 3% Above Treasury)	HMDA	2008	17.2	6.5	38%	38%
Median Home Value, Dollars	Census	2000	105,600	123,400	86%	65%
Median Wealth, 2005 Dollars	Pew	2002	7,932	88,651	9%	11%
Equity in Home, Dollars	Census	2002	49,000	79,200	62%	51%
Percent Investing in 401k, %	EBRI	2005	19.0	36.8	52%	73%
Percent Investing in IRA, %	EBRI	2005	8.5	27.7	31%	36%
Digital Divide (0.05)						
Households with Computer at Home, %	Census	2005	39.1	64.6	61%	69%
Households with the Internet, %	Census	2007	43.4	66.9	65%	68%
Adult Users with Broadband Access, %	Pew Internet & American Life Project	2009	68.0	65.0	105%	71%
Transportation (0.01)						
Car Ownership, %	Census	2002	78.8	88.4	89%	76%
Means of Transportation to Work: Drive Alone, %	ACS	2008	66.1	79.0	84%	89%
Means of Transportation to Work: Public Transportation, %	ACS	2008	8.2	2.9	36%	25%
Economic Weighted Index					61.0%	57.7%

HEALTH (25%)						
Death Rates & Life Expectancy (0.45)						
Age-Adjusted Death Rates (per 100,000)- All Causes	CDC	2006	564.0	777.0	138%	78%
Age-Adjusted Death Rates (per 100,000)- Male	CDC	2006	675.6	922.8	137%	74%
Age-Adjusted Death Rates (per 100,000)- Female	CDC	2006	468.6	660.0	141%	80%
Age-Adjusted Death Rates (per 100,000)- Heart Disease	CDC	2006	144.1	200.3	139%	76%
Ischemic Heart Disease	CDC	2006	106.4	136.0	128%	83%
Age-Adjusted Death Rates (per 100,000)- Stroke (Cerebrovascular)	CDC	2006	34.2	41.9	123%	67%
Age-Adjusted Death Rates (per 100,000)- Cancer	CDC	2006	118.0	184.6	156%	83%
Trachea, Bronchus, and Lung	CDC	2006	20.7	54.7	264%	94%
Colon, Rectum, and Anus	CDC	2006	12.6	17.0	135%	69%
Prostate (Male)	CDC	2006	18.1	21.9	121%	118%
Breast (Female)	CDC	2006	15.0	23.5	157%	124%
Age-Adjusted Death Rates (per 100,000)- Chronic Lower Respiratory	CDC	2006	17.3	44.4	257%	155%
Age-Adjusted Death Rates (per 100,000)-Influenza and Pneumonia	CDC	2006	15.0	17.8	119%	89%
Age-Adjusted Death Rates (per 100,000)-Chronic Liver Disease and Cirrhosis	CDC	2006	13.3	8.6	65%	121%
Age-Adjusted Death Rates (per 100,000)- Diabetes	CDC	2006	29.9	20.4	68%	44%
Age-Adjusted Death Rates (per 100,000)- HIV	CDC	2006	4.5	1.7	38%	9%
Unintentional Injuries	CDC	2006	31.5	42.1	134%	107%
Motor Vehicle-Related Injuries	CDC	2006	14.6	15.3	105%	96%
Age-Adjusted Death Rates (per 100,000)- Suicide	CDC	2006	5.3	13.2	249%	254%
Age-Adjusted Death Rates (per 100,000)- Suicide Males	CDC	2006	8.8	21.4	243%	223%
Age-Adjusted Death Rates (per 100,000)- Suicide Males Ages 15-24	CDC	2006	11.6	18.5	159%	175%

Different Source/Year for Hispanic-White Index than Black-White Index

2010 EQUALITY INDEX OF HISPANIC AMERICA	Source	Year	Hispanic	White	Index	Comparable Black-White Index
Age-Adjusted Death Rates (per 100,000)- Suicide Females	CDC	2006	1.8	5.6	311%	400%
Age-Adjusted Death Rates (per 100,000)- Suicide Females Ages 15-24	CDC	2006	2.6	3.5	135%	194%
Age-Adjusted Death Rates (per 100,000)- Homicide	CDC	2006	7.3	2.7	37%	12%
Age-Adjusted Death Rates (per 100,000)- Homicide Male	CDC	2006	11.7	3.6	31%	9%
Age-Adjusted Death Rates (per 100,000)- Homicide Males Ages 15-24	CDC	2006	31.0	4.7	15%	5%
Age-Adjusted Death Rates (per 100,000)- Homicide Female	CDC	2006	2.3	1.8	78%	27%
Age-Adjusted Death Rates (per 100,000)- Homicide Females Ages 15-24	CDC	2006	3.8	2.0	53%	21%
Age-Adjusted Death Rates (per 100,000) by Age Cohort: >1 Male	CDC	2006	640.7	621.9	97%	44%
Age-Adjusted Death Rates (per 100,000) by Age Cohort: 1-4 Male	CDC	2006	28.8	26.7	93%	57%
Age-Adjusted Death Rates (per 100,000) by Age Cohort: 5-14 Male	CDC	2006	16.4	16.2	99%	65%
Age-Adjusted Death Rates (per 100,000) by age cohort: 15-24 Male	CDC	2006	120.7	107.6	89%	63%
Age-Adjusted Death Rates (per 100,000) by Age Cohort: 25-34 Male	CDC	2006	112.7	141.1	125%	56%
Age-Adjusted Death Rates (per 100,000) by Age Cohort: 35-44 Male	CDC	2006	176.5	233.1	132%	59%
Age-Adjusted Death Rates (per 100,000) by Age Cohort: 45-54 Male	CDC	2006	403.8	515.1	128%	56%
Age-Adjusted Death Rates (per 100,000) by Age Cohort: 55-64 Male	CDC	2006	843.t6	1,064.0	126%	56%
Age-Adjusted Death Rates (per 100,000) by Age Cohort: 65-74 Male	CDC	2006	1,910.7	2,490.3	130%	68%
Age-Adjusted Death Rates (per 100,000) by Age Cohort: 75-84 Male	CDC	2006	4,492.6	6,278.3	140%	85%
Age-Adjusted Death Rates (per 100,000) by Age Cohort: 85+ Male	CDC	2006	9,435.5	14,841.1	157%	112%
Age-Adjusted Death Rates (per 100,000) by Age Cohort: >1 Female	CDC	2006	538.3	503.7	94%	42%
Age-Adjusted Death Rates (per 100,000) by Age Cohort: 1-4 Female	CDC	2006	24.0	23.2	97%	59%
Age-Adjusted Death Rates (per 100,000) by Age Cohort: 5-14 Female	CDC	2006	11.8	11.8	100%	68%
Age-Adjusted Death Rates (per 100,000) by Age Cohort: 15-24 Female	CDC	2006	35.2	42.9	122%	84%
Age-Adjusted Death Rates (per 100,000) by Age Cohort: 25-34 Female	CDC	2006	43.1	62.5	145%	59%
Age-Adjusted Death Rates (per 100,000) by Age Cohort: 35-44 Female	CDC	2006	87.1	136.3	156%	56%
Age-Adjusted Death Rates (per 100,000) by Age Cohort: 45-54 Female	CDC	2006	215.3	299.8	139%	55%
Age-Adjusted Death Rates (per 100,000) by Age Cohort: 55-64 Female	CDC	2006	486.5	668.0	137%	62%
Age-Adjusted Death Rates (per 100,000) by Age Cohort: 65-74 Female	CDC	2006	1,222.7	1,677.4	137%	75%
Age-Adjusted Death Rates (per 100,000) by Age Cohort: 75-84 Female	CDC	2006	3,222.9	4,460.7	138%	89%
Age-Adjusted Death Rates (per 100,000) by Age Cohort: 85+ Female	CDC	2006	8,803.5	13,150.7	149%	108%
Physical Condition (0.10)						
Overweight: 18+ Years, % of Population	CDC	2008	39.6	36.3	92%	103%
Overweight - Men 20 Years and Over, % of Population	CDC	2003-2006	46.3	39.4	85%	109%
Overweight - Women 20 Years and Over, % of Population	CDC	2003-2006	32.1	26.3	82%	100%
Obese, % of Population	CDC	2008	28.1	25.4	90%	69%
Obese - Men 20 Years and Over, % of Population	CDC	2003-2006	29.5	32.2	109%	91%
Obese - Women 20 Years and Over, % of Population	CDC	2003-2006	41.8	31.7	76%	60%
Diabetes: Physician Diagnosed in Ages 20+, % of Population	CDC	2003-2006	12.4	6.4	52%	48%
AIDS Cases per 100,000 Males Ages 13+	CDC	2007	31.0	10.6	34%	13%
AIDS Cases per 100,000 Females Ages 13+	CDC	2007	8.9	1.8	20%	5%
Substance Abuse (0.10)						

2010 EQUALITY INDEX OF HISPANIC AMERICA	Source	Year	Hispanic	White	Index	Comparable Black-White Index
Binge Alcohol (5 Drinks in 1 Day, 1x a Year) Ages 18+, % of Population	CDC	2007	17.3	24.4	141%	207%
Use of Illicit Drugs in the Past Month Ages 12 +, % of Population	CDC	2007	6.6	8.2	124%	86%
Tobacco: Both Cigarette & Cigar Ages 12+, % of Population	CDC	2007	22.7	30.7	135%	115%
Mental Health (0.02)						
Students Who Consider Suicide: Male, %	CDC	2007	10.7	10.2	95%	120%
Students Who Carry out Intent and Require Medical Attention: Male, %	CDC	2007	1.8	0.9	50%	36%
Students that Act on Suicidal Feeling: Male, %	CDC	2007	6.3	3.4	54%	62%
Students Who Consider Suicide: Female, %	CDC	2007	21.1	17.8	84%	99%
Students Who Carry out Intent and Require Medical Attention: Female, %	CDC	2007	3.9	2.1	54%	100%
Students That Act on Suicidal Feeling: Female, %	CDC	2007	14.0	7.7	55%	78%
Access to Care (0.05)						
Private Insurance Payment for Health Care: Under 65 Years Old, % of Distribution	CDC	2006	38.1	58.3	65%	71%
People Without Health Insurance, % of Population	Census	2008	30.7	10.8	35%	57%
People 18 to 64 Without A Usual Source of Health Insurance, % of Adults	Census	2008	40.8	14.6	36%	57%
People in Poverty Without a Usual Source of Health Insurance, % of Adults	Census	2008	59.0	38.5	65%	101%
Population Under 65 Covered by Medicaid, % of Population	CDC	2007	24.7	8.5	34%	31%
Elderly Health Care (0.03)						
Population over 65 Covered by Medicaid, % of Population	CDC	2007	24.4	5.7	23%	30%
Medicare Expenditures per Beneficiary, Dollars	CDC	2006	13,503	15,587	115%	87%
Pregnancy Issues (0.04)						
Prenatal Care Begins in 1st Trimester	CDC	2006	75.7	88.1	86%	86%
Prenatal Care Begins in 3rd Trimester	CDC	2006	5.0	2.3	46%	40%
Percent of Births to Mothers 18 and Under	CDC	2006	5.2	2.0	38%	32%
Percent of Live Births to Unmarried Mothers	CDC	2006	49.9	26.6	53%	38%
Infant Mortality Rates Among Mothers 20 Years of Age and Over, by Education						
Less than 12 years Education	CDC	2005	5.2	6.5	125%	47%
12 Years Education	CDC	2005	5.4	6.6	122%	48%
13 Years or More Education	CDC	2005	4.6	4.2	91%	38%
Mothers Who Smoked Cigarettes During Pregnancy, %	CDC	2006	2.6	13.3	512%	168%
Low Birth Weight, % of Live Births	CDC	2006	7.0	7.3	105%	52%
Very Low Birth Weight, % of Live Births	CDC	2006	1.2	1.2	101%	38%
Reproduction Issues (0.01)						
Abortions, per 100 Live Births	CDC	2005	20.5	15.8	77%	34%
Women Using Contraception, % of Population	CDC	2002	59.0	64.6	91%	89%
Delivery Issues (0.10)						
All Infant Deaths: Neonatal and Post, per 1000 Live Births	CDC	2005	5.6	5.8	104%	43%
Neonatal Deaths, per 1000 Live Births	CDC	2005	3.9	3.7	95%	41%
PostNeonatal Deaths, per 1000 Live Births	CDC	2005	1.8	2.1	117%	47%
Maternal Mortality, per 100,000 Live Births	CDC	2006	8.8	8.0	91%	28%
Children's Health (0.10)						
Babies Breastfed, %	CDC	1999-2001	76.0	68.7	111%	77%

Different Source/Year for Hispanic-White Index than Black-White Index

2010 EQUALITY INDEX OF HISPANIC AMERICA	Source	Year	Hispanic	White	Index	Comparable Black-White Index
Children Without a Health Care Visit in Past 12 Months (Up to 6 Years Old), %	CDC	2006-2007	9.1	6.1	67%	130%
Vaccinations of Children Below Poverty: Combined Vacc. Series 4:3:1:3, % of Children 19-35 Months	CDC	2007	78.0	70.0	111%	106%
Uninsured Children, %	Census	2008	17.2	6.7	39%	63%
Overweight Boys 6-11 Years Old, % of Population	CDC	2003-2006	27.5	15.5	56%	83%
Overweight Girls 6-11 Years Old, % of Population	CDC	2003-2006	19.7	14.4	73%	60%
AIDS Cases per 100,000 All Children Under 13	CDC	2007	2.0	5.0	250%	24%
Health Weighted Index					103.4%	73.2%

EDUCATION (25%)

Quality (.25)

Teacher Quality (.10)

	Source	Year	Hispanic	White	Index	Comparable Black-White Index
Middle Grades - Teacher Lacking at Least a College Minor in Subject Taught (High vs. Low Minority Schools), %	ET	2000	49.0	40.0	85%	85%
HS - Teacher Lacking an Undergraduate Major in Subject Taught (High vs. Low Minority Schools), %	ET	2000	28.0	21.0	91%	91%
Per Student Funding (High vs. Low Poverty Districts), Dollars	ET	2004	5,937	7,244	82%	82%
Teachers With <3 Years Experience (High vs. Low Minority Schools) , %	NCES	2000	21.0	10.0	48%	48%
Distribution of Underprepared Teachers (High vs. Low Minority Schools), % (California Only)	SRI	2007-2008	7.0	2.0	29%	29%

Course Quality (0.15)

	Source	Year	Hispanic	White	Index	Comparable Black-White Index
College Completion, % of All Entrants	ET	1999	61.0	73.0	84%	62%
College Completion, % of Entrants with Strong HS Curriculum (Algebra II Plus Other Courses)	ET	1999	79.0	86.0	92%	87%
HS Students: Enrolled in Chemistry, %	NCES	2005	59.2	67.1	88%	95%
HS Students: Enrolled in Algebra 2, %	NCES	2005	62.7	71.2	88%	97%
Students Taking: Precalculus, %	CB	2009	45.3	55.0	82%	65%
Students Taking: Calculus, %	CB	2009	19.3	30.0	64%	47%
Students Taking: Physics, %	CB	2009	47.0	54.0	87%	81%
Students Taking: English Honors Course, %	CB	2009	35.0	43.0	81%	72%

Attainment (0.30)

	Source	Year	Hispanic	White	Index	Comparable Black-White Index
Graduation Rates, 2-year Institutions, %	NCES	2002	33.6	33.8	99%	80%
Graduation Rates, 4-year Institutions, %	NCES	1999	46.7	58.9	79%	69%
NCAA Div. I College Freshmen Graduating Within 6 Years, %	NCAA	2001-2002	53.0	65.0	82%	69%
Degrees Earned: Associate, % of population Aged 18-24 Years	NCES	2007	1.7	2.7	62%	76%
Degrees Earned: Bachelor's, % of Population Aged 18-29 Years	NCES	2007	1.3	3.6	35%	55%
Degrees Earned: Master's, % of population aged 18-34 Years	NCES	2007	0.7	0.9	73%	66%
Educational Attainment: At Least High School (25 Years. and Over), % of Population	Census	2008	62.3	91.5	68%	91%
Educational Attainment: At Least Bachelor's (25 Years. and Over), % of Population	Census	2008	13.3	32.6	41%	60%
Degree Holders, % Distribution, by Field						

2010 EQUALITY INDEX OF HISPANIC AMERICA	Source	Year	Hispanic	White	Index	Comparable Black-White Index
Agriculture/Forestry	NCES	2001	1.1	1.2	96%	56%
Art/Architecture	NCES	2001	4.8	2.9	166%	114%
Business/Management	NCES	2001	19.5	18.1	108%	108%
Communications	NCES	2001	3.3	2.4	140%	135%
Computer and Information Sciences	NCES	2001	2.6	2.2	119%	177%
Education	NCES	2001	10.7	15.3	70%	100%
Engineering	NCES	2001	7.9	7.7	103%	47%
English/Literature	NCES	2001	3.1	3.3	95%	80%
Foreign Languages	NCES	2001	1.7	0.9	202%	96%
Health Sciences	NCES	2001	4.4	4.5	98%	120%
Liberal Arts/Humanities	NCES	2001	4.7	6.1	77%	75%
Mathematics/Statistics	NCES	2001	2.4	1.4	167%	169%
Natural Sciences	NCES	2001	4.9	5.6	88%	106%
Philosophy/Religion/Theology	NCES	2001	1.8	1.3	132%	70%
Pre-Professional	NCES	2001	2.0	1.1	182%	146%
Psychology	NCES	2001	5.0	3.9	129%	126%
Social Sciences/History	NCES	2001	4.7	4.9	95%	165%
Other Fields	NCES	2001	15.4	17.2	89%	76%
Scores (.25)						
Preschool 10% of Total Scores (0.015)						
Children's School Readiness Skills (Ages 3-5), % with 3 or 4 Skills* *Recognizes all letters, counts to 20 or higher, writes name, reads or pretends to read	NCES	2005	26.0	46.8	55%	94%
Elementary 40% of Total Scores (0.06)						
Average Scale Score in U.S. History, 8th Graders	NCES	2006	248	273	91%	89%
Average Scale Score in U.S. History, 4th Graders	NCES	2006	194	223	87%	86%
Average Scale Score in Math, 8th Graders	NCES	2007	265	291	91%	89%
Average Scale Score in Math, 4th Graders	NCES	2007	227	248	91%	90%
Average Scale Score in Reading, 8th Graders	NCES	2007	247	272	91%	90%
Average Scale Score in Reading, 4th Graders	NCES	2007	205	231	89%	88%
Average Scale Score in Science, 8th Graders	NCES	2005	129	160	81%	78%
Average Scale Score in Science, 4th Graders	NCES	2005	133	162	82%	80%
Writing Proficiency at or Above Basic, 8th Graders, % of Students	NCES	2007	80	93	86%	87%
Writing Proficiency at or Above Basic, 4th Graders, % of Students	NCES	2002	77	90	85%	85%
High School 50% of Total Scores (0.075)						
Writing Proficiency at or Above Basic, 12th Graders, % of Students	NCES	2007	71	86	83%	80%
Average Scale Score in Science, 12th Graders	NCES	2005	128	156	82%	77%
Average Scale Score in U.S. History, 12th graders	NCES	2006	275	297	93%	91%
Average Scale Score in Reading, 12th Graders	NCES	2005	272	293	93%	91%
High School GPA's for Those Taking the SAT	CB	2008	3.2	3.4	94%	89%
SAT Reasoning Test - Mean Scores	CB	2009	1,361	1,581	86%	81%
Mathematics, Joint	CB	2009	461	536	86%	79%
Mathematics, Male	CB	2009	481	555	87%	78%

Different Source/Year for Hispanic-White Index than Black-White Index

2010 EQUALITY INDEX OF HISPANIC AMERICA	Source	Year	Hispanic	White	Index	Comparable Black-White Index
Mathematics, Female	CB	2009	445	520	86%	81%
Critical Reading, Joint	CB	2009	454	528	86%	81%
Critical Reading, Male	CB	2009	459	530	87%	80%
Critical Reading, Female	CB	2009	450	526	86%	82%
Writing, Joint	CB	2009	447	517	86%	81%
Writing, Male	CB	2009	443	509	87%	81%
Writing, Female	CB	2009	449	524	86%	82%
ACT - Average Composite Score	ACT	2009	19	22	84%	59%
Enrollment (0.10)						
School Enrollment: Ages 3-34, % of Population	Census	2008	51.9	56.7	91%	102%
Preprimary School Enrollment	Census	2008	54.7	66.5	82%	96%
3 and 4 Years Old	Census	2008	43.6	56.0	78%	98%
5 and 6 Years Old	Census	2008	91.8	94.9	97%	98%
7 to 13 Years Old	Census	2008	97.9	98.9	99%	100%
14 and 15 Years Old	Census	2008	98.7	98.8	100%	99%
16 and 17 Years Old	Census	2008	93.8	95.9	98%	98%
18 and 19 Years Old	Census	2008	55.1	70.0	79%	85%
20 and 21 Years Old	Census	2008	32.1	55.8	58%	72%
22 to 24 Years Old	Census	2008	19.8	30.3	65%	82%
25 to 29 Years Old	Census	2008	9.2	13.3	69%	111%
30 to 34 Years Old	Census	2008	4.2	6.9	61%	167%
35 and Over	Census	2008	2.2	1.8	123%	159%
College Enrollment (Graduate or Undergraduate): Ages 14 and Over, % of Population	Census	2008	5.1	6.5	78%	106%
14 to 17 Years Old	Census	2008	1.7	1.2	141%	113%
18 to 19 Years Old	Census	2008	34.3	55.0	62%	65%
20 to 21 Years Old	Census	2008	29.0	54.9	53%	67%
22 to 24 Years Old	Census	2008	18.0	30.1	60%	81%
25 to 29 Years Old	Census	2008	8.7	13.0	67%	102%
30 to 34 Years Old	Census	2008	3.5	6.9	51%	159%
35 Years Old and Over	Census	2008	1.9	1.7	114%	157%
College Enrollment Rate as a Percent of All 18- to 24-Year-Old High School Completers, %	NCES	2007	39.2	47.8	82%	84%
Adult Education Participation, % of Adult Population	NCES	2004-05	38.0	46.0	83%	100%
Student Status & Risk Factors (.10)						
High School Dropouts: Status Dropouts, % (Not Completed HS and Not Enrolled, Regardless of When Dropped)	Census	2006	26.2	10.8	41%	83%
Children in Poverty, %	Census	2008	30.6	10.6	35%	31%
Children in All Families Below Poverty Level, %	Census	2008	30.3	10.0	33%	29%
Children in Families Below Poverty Level (Female Householder, No Spouse present), %	Census	2008	51.9	31.6	61%	61%
Children (under 18) with a Disability, %	Census	2008	3.4	4.0	117%	81%
Public School Students (K-12): Repeated grade, %	NCES	2003	10.6	8.2	77%	48%

2010 EQUALITY INDEX OF HISPANIC AMERICA	Source	Year	Hispanic	White	Index	Comparable Black-White Index
Public School Students (K-12): Suspended, %	NCES	2003	10.4	8.8	85%	45%
Public School Students (K-12): Expelled, %	NCES	2003	1.4	1.4	100%	28%
Center-Based Child Care of Preschool Children, %	NCES	2005	43.4	59.1	136%	89%
Parental Care Only of Preschool Children, %	NCES	2005	38.0	24.1	158%	81%
Teacher Stability: Remained in Public School, High vs. Low Minority Schools, %	NCES	2005	79.7	85.9	93%	93%
Teacher Stability: Remained in Private School, High vs. Low Minority Schools, %	NCES	2005	72.7	82.8	88%	88%
Zero Days Missed in School Year, % of 10th Graders	NCES	2002	14.2	13.0	110%	127%
3+ Days Late to School, % of 10th Graders	NCES	2002	44.8	31.5	70%	68%
Never Cut Classes, % of 10th Graders	NCES	2002	56.3	72.9	77%	89%
Home Literacy Activities (Age 3 to 5)						
Read to Three or More Times a Week	NCES	2005	71.9	91.9	78%	85%
Told a Story at Least Once a Month	NCES	2005	49.8	53.3	93%	102%
Taught Words or Numbers Three or More Times a Week	NCES	2005	74.3	75.7	98%	107%
Visited a Library at Least Once in Last Month	NCES	2005	31.8	44.9	71%	98%
Education Weighted Index					76.5%	78.1%

SOCIAL JUSTICE (10%)

Equality Before the Law (0.70)

	Source	Year	Hispanic	White	Index	Comparable
Stopped While Driving, %	BJS	2005	8.9	8.9	100%	110%
Speeding	BJS	2002	44.4	57.0	128%	114%
Vehicle Defect	BJS	2002	14.0	8.7	62%	84%
Roadside Check for Drinking Drivers	BJS	2002	1.6	1.3	81%	118%
Record Check	BJS	2002	7.8	11.3	145%	65%
Seatbelt Violation	BJS	2002	5.5	4.4	80%	126%
Illegal Turn/Lane Change	BJS	2002	5.7	4.5	79%	88%
Stop Sign/Light Violation	BJS	2002	11.2	6.5	58%	110%
Other	BJS	2002	6.2	4.0	65%	108%
Incarceration Rate: Prisoners per 100,000	BJS	2008	1,125	334	30%	16%
Incarceration Rate: Prisoners per 100,000 People - Male	BJS	2008	1,200	487	41%	15%
Incarceration Rate: Prisoners per 100,000 People - Female	BJS	2008	75	50	67%	34%

Victimization & Mental Anguish (0.30)

Homicide Rate per 100,000 - Male	CDC	2006	13.1	3.6	27%	9%
Homicide Rate per 100,000 - Female	CDC	2006	2.4	1.8	75%	27%
Hate Crimes Victims, Rate per 100,000	USDJ	2007	1.8	0.4	21%	4%
Victims of Violent Crimes, Rate per 100,000	BJS	2008	16.4	18.1	110%	70%
High School Students Carrying Weapons on School Property	CDC	2007	7.3	5.3	73%	88%
High School Students Carrying Weapons Anywhere	CDC	2007	18.5	18.2	98%	106%
Firearm-Related Death Rates per 100,000: Males, All Ages	CDC	2006	13.8	15.7	113%	37%
Ages 1-14	CDC	2006	1.1	0.7	64%	29%

Different Source/Year for Hispanic-White Index than Black-White Index

2010 EQUALITY INDEX OF HISPANIC AMERICA	Source	Year	Hispanic	White	Index	Comparable Black-White Index
Ages 15-24	CDC	2006	34.5	13.9	40%	15%
Ages 25-44	CDC	2006	17.7	17.1	97%	26%
Ages 25-34	CDC	2006	21.5	16.3	76%	17%
Ages 35-44	CDC	2006	13.1	17.8	136%	45%
Ages 45-64	CDC	2006	8.6	19.5	227%	99%
Age 65 and Older	CDC	2006	7.7	27.3	357%	203%
Firearm-Related Death Rates per 100,000: Females, All Ages	CDC	2006	1.5	2.8	188%	67%
Ages 1-14	CDC	2006	0.4	0.3	83%	33%
Ages 15-24	CDC	2006	2.7	2.2	81%	28%
Ages 25-44	CDC	2006	2.3	3.8	163%	52%
Ages 25-34	CDC	2006	2.5	3.1	123%	35%
Ages 35-44	CDC	2006	2.1	4.4	208%	75%
Ages 45-64	CDC	2006	1.4	4.2	310%	158%
Age 65 and Older	CDC	2006	0.4	2.2	491%	208%
Social Justice Weighted Index					62.4%	76.8%

CIVIC ENGAGEMENT (10%)						
Democratic Process (0.4)						
Registered Voters, % of Citizen Population	Census	2008	59.4	73.5	81%	95%
Actually Voted, % of Citizen Population	Census	2008	49.9	66.1	75%	98%
Community Participation (0.3)						
Percent of Population Volunteering for Military Reserves, %	USDD	2007	0.5	1.0	48%	90%
Volunteerism, %	BLS	2008	14.4	27.9	52%	68%
Civic and Political	BLS	2008	3.1	5.6	55%	77%
Educational or Youth Service	BLS	2008	34.5	26.1	132%	88%
Environmental or Animal Care	BLS	2008	1.1	2.2	50%	14%
Hospital or Other Health	BLS	2008	5.2	8.5	61%	74%
Public Safety	BLS	2008	0.6	1.4	43%	14%
Religious	BLS	2008	38.5	33.9	114%	137%
Social or Community Service	BLS	2008	9.6	13.8	70%	92%
Unpaid Volunteering of Young Adults	NCES	2000	30.7	32.2	95%	127%
Collective Bargaining (0.2)						
Members of Unions, % of Employed	BLS	2008	10.6	12.2	87%	119%
Represented by Unions, % of Employed	BLS	2008	11.7	13.5	87%	117%
Governmental Employment (0.1)						
Federal Executive Branch (Nonpostal) Employment, % of Adult Population	OPM	2006	0.5	0.8	59%	146%
State and Local Government Employment, %	EEOC	2005	1.9	2.6	74%	162%
Civic Engagement Weighted Index					71.9%	102.2%

Due to data availability, the 2010 Equality Index of Hispanic America does not include all the variables that were used to calculate the 2010 Equality Index of Black America. Therefore, weights were redistributed among the available variables and a comparable Black-White index was calculated solely to provide a consistent comparison between blacks and Hispanics.

Putting Americans Back to Work:
The National Urban League's Plan for Creating Jobs

MARC H. MORIAL, VALERIE RAWLSTON WILSON, PH.D., CY RICHARDSON AND TERRY CLARK

In October 2009, news that the national unemployment rate exceeded ten percent for the first time since the early 1980s presented a sobering wake-up call to the leadership of this country. With over 27 million Americans underemployed (meaning either unemployed, marginally attached to the labor force or working part-time for economic reasons), President Obama convened a Jobs Summit during the first week in December.

While this spike in unemployment rightfully attracted national attention, little was made of double-digit unemployment rates that had been a reality for communities of color since the previous summer—for African Americans since August 2008 and for Latinos since February 2009. In fact, the jobless recovery of 2001 had left the African-American unemployment rate at or near 10 percent since December 2001.

More than a year before national unemployment reached 10.2% in October 2009, the National Urban League (NUL) had been on the front lines with families facing tremendous economic obstacles. This is evidenced by the 74 percent increase in demand for workforce development, business development and housing counseling services offered through the Urban League's more than 100 affiliates between 2006 and 2008. In response, the National Urban League went on record in the fall of 2009 to draw attention to the deepening unemployment crisis in urban America and to call for a second stimulus plan that would invest in direct job creation and training for the very communities NUL interacts with and serves everyday.

In November 2009, the National Urban League introduced *The National Urban League's Plan for Putting Americans Back to Work*, a six-point plan for job creation that was detailed in a letter addressed to Lawrence Summers, Director of the National Economic Council, House Speaker Nancy Pelosi, Senate Majority Leader Harry Reid and Congressional Black Caucus Chair Barbara Lee. The bold six-point plan proposes a direct investment of $168 billion over 2 years to address the most urgent needs of American families in economic crisis by investing in direct job creation, job training for the

chronically unemployed, greater access to credit for small businesses and additional counseling relief for those caught in the backlog of the foreclosure process. The plan also proposes tax incentives for clean energy equipment manufacturers who employ individuals in the targeted communities. The plan proposes to do these things in the following ways:

Investing in policies that help to increase employment and boost the economy will actually help to reduce the deficit.

① **Fund Direct Job Creation** by offering financial support to cities, counties, states, universities, community colleges and non-profit community-based organizations to hire the personnel necessary to provide critical services in communities across the nation. Eligibility for support will be based on local unemployment rates with a focus on the long-term unemployed. At least twice in American history, the government has responded to high rates of unemployment with investments in direct job creation—the 1935 *Works Progress Administration* when nearly one-fourth of the labor force was out of work, and the *Emergency Jobs and Unemployment Assistance Act of 1974* which established Title VI of CETA as a temporary countercyclical employment program at a time when unemployment was quickly approaching 9 percent. We propose an investment of $150 billion to create 3 million jobs, a number that represents only half of the current unemployed with a high school diploma or less.

② **Expand and Expedite the Small Business Administration's Community Express Loan Program** through a reduction of the interest rate to 1 percent targeted for those businesses located in areas where the local unemployment rate exceeds the state average. A ten-fold expansion of the program (from $1 billion to $10 billion) should make credit available to an additional 50,000 small businesses nationwide.

③ **Create Green Empowerment Zones** in areas where at least 50 percent of the population has an unemployment rate that is higher than the state average. Manufacturers of solar panels and wind turbines that open plants in high unemployment areas will for a period of three years, be eligible for a zero federal income tax rate and a zero capital gains tax under the condition that they hire and retain for a minimum of three years at least half of their workforce from the local area.

④ **Expand the Hiring of Housing Counselors Nationwide** by investing $500 million to fund housing counseling agencies nationwide to help delinquent borrowers work with their loan servicers to secure more affordable mortgages. Over the past 18 months, more than $400 million in federal funds have been invested by the Administration to help mitigate the mortgage crisis through housing counseling. According to a recent report by the Urban Institute, borrowers facing foreclosure

are 60% more likely to hold onto their homes if they receive counseling and receive loan modifications with average monthly payments that are $454 lower than those who did not see counselors.

⑤ **Expand the Youth Summer Jobs Program** for 2010 by investing $5-7 billion to employ 5 million teens. While the unemployment rate for African-American youth is over 40 percent, the employment population ratio makes clearer the desperate situation faced by many urban youth. Since the late 1990s, this number has declined from a high of 33 percent down to an average of 15 percent and labor force participation for this group reached a record low of 26 percent in 2009. A critical factor in eliminating racial and socio-economic disparities in unemployment is providing a solid foundation upon which African-American youth can build positive future labor market expectations and experiences.

⑥ **Create 100 Urban Jobs Academies** to implement an expansion of the Urban Youth Empowerment Program (UYEP) to employ and train the chronically unemployed. UYEP, a four year demonstration project created in partnership with the U.S. Department of Labor in 2004, is a youth career preparation initiative designed for at-risk, out-of-school and adjudicated youth and young adults between the ages of 18 and 24. With 27 Urban League affiliate sites and a total of $29.3 million, the program served 3,900 youth, 65 percent of whom either had job placements (paying an average wage of $9.32/hour) or completed their high school diploma or GED. Two hundred participants were placed in postsecondary schools or colleges upon completion of their secondary education. Scaling this program up to 100 sites would more than triple the program at a cost of $108.5 million.

Most economists agree that the pace of economic recovery and job growth will be slow and that less-educated, low-wage workers and minorities are often the last to experience the effects of even a more rapid economic recovery. Despite such dire projections, there are those who oppose major spending for job creation measures, often citing concerns over the growing budget deficit. However, this is often a skewed argument, focusing heavily on the new spending needed to create jobs and stimulate the economy to the neglect of the high and growing costs of forgone tax revenues and expenditures on income security programs like unemployment insurance and food stamps. For example, well over half of the Congressional Budget Office's change in the projected baseline budget deficit between January 2008 and August 2009 ($778 billion of the total $1,380 billion increase) was due to the declining economy.[1] Therefore, investing in policies that help to increase employment and boost the economy will actually help to reduce the deficit by stemming the losses in tax revenues and rising safety net spending that have resulted from the largest economic crisis since the Great Depression.

NOTES

[1] Bivens, Josh. "BUDGETING FOR RECOVERY: The Need to Increase the Federal Deficit to Revive a Weak Economy". Economic Policy Institute, Briefing Paper #253. January 6, 2010. *http://epi.3cdn.net/1616707e0 c784d8134_4nm6becsb.pdf*

African Americans & the Green Revolution: A Report from the National Urban League Policy Institute

VALERIE RAWLSTON WILSON, PH.D.

As the United States economy nears the end of what has been the longest recession in post-World War II history,[1] the question on everyone's mind seems to be, what will be the engine that drives economic expansion into the future? Put differently, what will be the next impetus for innovation, a force that has commonly propelled the evolution of the American economy from one generation to the next? Much like what information technology (minus the bubble) did for job growth during the 1990s, already some are hoping that the "greening of America" will offer a much needed post-millenial boost to the American economy, particularly as it pertains to jobs.

The term "green" is used to define products or services that have a positive impact on energy and/or environmental sustainability.[2] Though the idea of green living was once reserved primarily for diehard environmentalists, today the green lifestyle is promoted in almost every facet of mainstream American society, including national economic policy and our First Lady's White House garden. In fact, the American Recovery and Reinvestment Act (ARRA) of 2009 included $85 billion in direct spending and tax cuts for energy and transportation-related programs intended to jump start America's transition to a green economy by creating jobs and encouraging private investment in a more energy-efficient economy.

This report considers some of the estimates and projections from an ever-growing body of literature on the green economy and green jobs in order to evaluate employment opportunities for African American workers, a group that has persistently experienced unemployment rates twice that of their white counterparts. We begin with a working definition of green jobs as outlined by the Workforce Information Council (WIC) Green Jobs Study Group. Using Current Population Survey data, we evaluate trends in unemployment over the past two years for a previously defined set of representative green economy occupations and explore these trends in light of national and state-level growth projections for the green economy. Based on this information, we examine the role of the National Urban League in facilitating the transition to a green economy for the communities we serve and conclude with a discussion of current legislation and policies.

Defining Green Jobs and the Green Economy
Despite extensive usage of the term "green" to define all things (even remotely) eco-friendly or energy efficient, the discussion about what constitutes a green job continues to be ongoing and a definitive answer remains a work in progress. In October 2009, the WIC Green Jobs Study Group released its Final Report on *Measurement and Analysis of Employment in the Green Economy*. In this report they propose the following working definition of green jobs based on a review of existing green concepts and definitions from 43 studies:

A green job is one in which the work is essential to products or services that improve energy efficiency, expand the use of renewable energy, or support environmental sustainability. The job involves work in any of these green economic activity categories:

» *Renewable Energy and Alternative Fuels*

» *Energy Efficiency and Conservation*

» *Pollution, Waste and Greenhouse Gas (GHG) Management, Prevention, and Reduction*

» *Environmental Cleanup and Remediation and Waste Cleanup and Mitigation*

» *Sustainable Agriculture and Natural Resource Conservation*

» *Education, Regulation, Compliance, Public Awareness, and Training and Energy Trading.*[3]

Though the exact categories used to identify different types of green jobs vary from one study to the next, each of them describes a green job as being connected to a green economic activity. There is also general consensus among researchers that many of the "new" jobs will involve a restructuring of currently existing occupations and skills to meet the demands of a more energy efficient economy. Additionally, some green job definitions characterize the quality of jobs as "good," "family-supporting" or "well-paid career track,"[4] suggesting a focus on new jobs that are both environmentally- and economically-sustainable.

For the purpose of this analysis, Current Population Survey (CPS) data are used to identify representative green occupations according to the methodology used in the Political Economy Research Institute's (PERI) report titled *Job Opportunities for the Green Economy* which involved using data from the Bureau of Economic Analysis and the Bureau of Labor Statistics (BLS) to identify currently existing industries and occupations that would be "most affected" by investments in six strategies for attacking global warming. These six strategies are: building retrofitting,

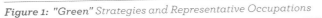

Figure 1: *"Green" Strategies and Representative Occupations*

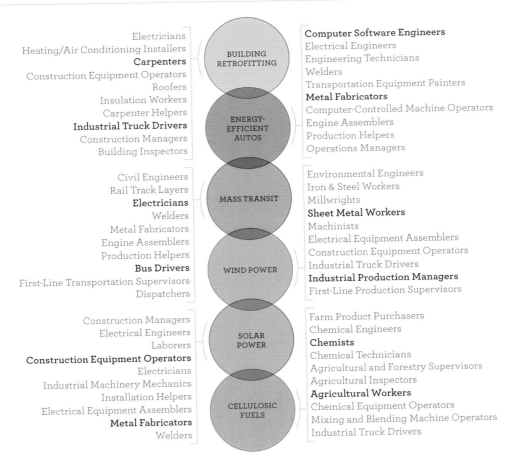

mass transit, energy-efficient automobiles, wind power, solar power and cellulosic biofuels. Based on these six strategies, PERI researchers identify forty-five currently existing occupations as representative green economy jobs.[5] *Figure 1* provides a listing of these six green strategies along with the corresponding representative occupations. While this is by no means an exhaustive list of all green economy activities and jobs (for example, the list excludes support occupations), each of these representative activities and jobs are all included in at least one of the Green Economic Activity categories outlined by the WIC Green Jobs Study Group. It is important to note that because the measurement and classification of green jobs is evolving along with the green economy, CPS data currently does not include a green industry classification. Therefore, any related statistics are representative of all employment in these occupations, not just green employment.

This definition provides a good framework for evaluating labor market conditions and opportunities that will likely be available to today's workforce because the strategies the PERI researchers emphasize are geared toward opportunities for near-term economic growth and include familiar jobs accessible to individuals with a wide range of skills and levels of education. For example, according to the Bureau of Labor Statistics, 20% of the occupations identified as representative green economy occupations are currently accessible to individuals with only a high school diploma; 49% are accessible to individuals with a high school diploma or some college; and 22% require a college degree *(Figure 2)*. While some specialized training will be required to convert many of these occupations to their specific green economy applications, BLS estimates that the majority of occupations accessible to those with a high school diploma or some college already require some short- to moderate-term on-the-job training.

Recent Trends in Employment and Wages
Applying the above green job identification strategy to the December 2007 Current Population Survey, which corresponds with

Figure 2: Distribution of Representative "Green" Occupations by Educational Cluster

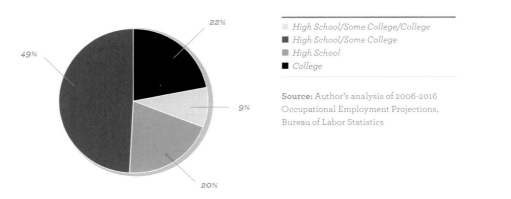

- High School/Some College/College
- High School/Some College
- High School
- College

Source: Author's analysis of 2006-2016 Occupational Employment Projections, Bureau of Labor Statistics

Figure 3: *Distribution of Representative "Green" Occupations by Race & Ethnicity (12/07)*

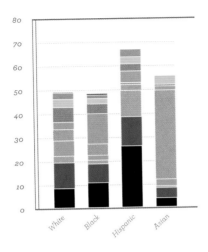

■ *Installation Helpers*
■ *Construction Equipment Operators*
■ *Welders*
■ *Electricians*
■ *Industrial Truck Drivers*
■ *Computer Software Engineers*
■ *Operations Managers*
■ *Agricultural Workers*
■ *Carpenters*
■ *Laborers*

Source: Author's analysis of 2006-2016 Occupational Employment Projections and Current Population Survey, December 2007, Bureau of Labor Statistics

the peak of the last economic expansion, we find that 7.7% of the labor force was in a representative green economy occupation. Males were more likely than females to be employed in representative green economy jobs—14% compared to 2%, respectively—as most of these occupations are in the construction (42%) and manufacturing (22%) industries which tend to be male dominated. A racial breakdown of these occupations reveals that Hispanics had the largest concentration at 11.4%, followed by Asians (7%), whites (7.4%) and African Americans (5.5%). As *Figure 3* illustrates, racial and ethnic minorities also tend to be less evenly distributed across representative green economy occupations than whites.

Among the ten green economy related occupations projected by BLS to grow the most between 2006 and 2016, Hispanics were most heavily concentrated in construction laborer occupations (26%) while African Americans were highly concentrated in industrial truck driving (13%) and construction labor (11%), and Asians are widely represented in computer software engineering (38%). These racial and ethnic breakdowns are important because they also have implications in terms of wages. For example, the highest hourly wages are paid to operations managers ($51.91/hour) and computer software engineers ($42.26/hour), followed by the more skilled trades such as electricians ($23.98/hour) and carpenters ($20.64/hour).[6] Relative to each group's distribution across all representative green economy occupations, nearly 28% of whites were in one of these higher paying occupations compared to 19% of African Americans and Hispanics. While these differences may be partially reflective of differences in educational attainment and training, research published in *The State of Black America 2006* offers evidence of patterns of exclusion from more desired and higher paying occupations even for African Americans with the requisite educational qualifications[7].

Representative Green Jobs During the Recession

Between the start of the recession in December 2007 and August 2009, the purported end of the recession as indicated by positive GDP growth, the construction industry lost a net of 1.4 million jobs while the manufacturing industry shed 2 million jobs.[8] Given the high concentration of green economy jobs within these industries, unemployment rates among representative green economy occupations exceeded that of all other occupations throughout the duration of the recession (Figure 4). While private job losses began to moderate in the spring, going from an average of nearly -670,000 economy-wide between January 2009 and April 2009 to -312,000 in May 2009, by August, unemployment in representative green occupations still exceeded the national unemployment rate by 3 percentage points, representing 2.2 million unemployed people and an additional 1.2 million who were marginally attached

or working part-time for economic reasons.[9] Between December 2007 and May 2009, unemployment among representative green occupations accelerated faster than the national average because job losses were occurring predominantly in construction and manufacturing in response to the rapidly deflating housing bubble. By comparison, the difference in the unemployment rate was less than one percentage point at the end of 2006 when unemployment was at its lowest level.

When we observe trends in representative green job unemployment by race and ethnicity during the recession, some interesting patterns emerge (Figure 5). For example, at the start of the recession, the unemployment rates of African Americans and Hispanics in these occupations were similar (8.4% and 9.2%, respectively). However, the gap widened considerably over the course of the recession with the African American unemployment rate increasing by 91% between December 2007 and December 2008, compared to a 27% increase for

Figure 4: *Representative "Green" vs. Non-"Green" Unemployment Rate (not seasonally adjusted)*

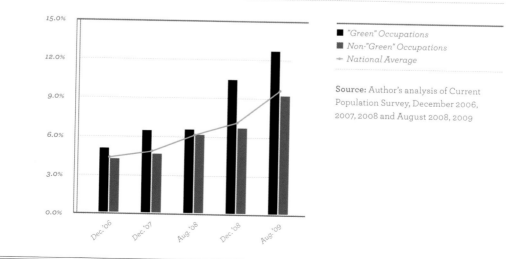

■ "Green" Occupations
■ Non-"Green" Occupations
→ National Average

Source: Author's analysis of Current Population Survey, December 2006, 2007, 2008 and August 2008, 2009

Hispanics. By August 2009, when GDP began to increase again, the unemployment rates for African American and Hispanic workers in representative green economy occupations had converged again at 18% compared to the 4 percentage point gap that existed the previous August. The unemployment rates of Asians and Whites in representative green economy occupations had also converged by August 2009—11% for whites and 10% for Asians—as a result of unemployment rates for Asians rising much faster than those of their white counterparts, despite the fact that Asians in these professions had much lower unemployment rates than whites throughout the earlier months of the recession.

As *Figure 6* shows, these changes in unemployment rates coincide with the fact that for both African Americans and Asians, the number of persons vying for these jobs increased between December 2007 and December 2008 as the number of jobless persons in this segment of the labor force

increased over this period of time. For whites and Hispanics, people were actually leaving this segment of the labor force. Between August 2008 and August 2009, all groups saw a decline in the number of people in this segment of labor force. However, African Americans were exiting at a 5-8 times faster rate than other groups while the number of jobless African Americans increased at a much slower pace, suggesting that the majority of those leaving the labor force were people without jobs. On the other hand, the number of unemployed Asians increased dramatically between August 2008 and August 2009 relative to the rate of decline in the number of people seeking employment.

The excessively high rates of unemployment for persons in representative green economy occupations, particularly among African American and Hispanic workers, suggest an available pool of skilled workers who can fill jobs created by the emerging green economy that must not be overlooked. In fact, as workers with relatively recent experience in the jobs that

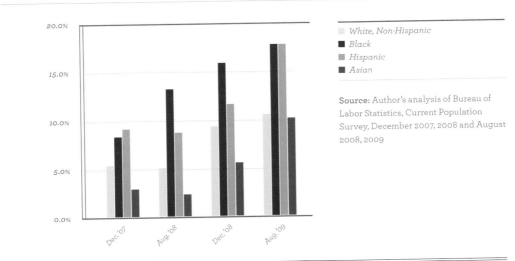

Figure 5: *Unemployment Rate in "Green" Occupations (not seasonally adjusted)*

White, Non-Hispanic
Black
Hispanic
Asian

Source: Author's analysis of Bureau of Labor Statistics, Current Population Survey, December 2007, 2008 and August 2008, 2009

are likely to be in high demand for the green economy, these workers should be among the easiest to employ quickly.

Job Growth Projections
for the Green Economy

The discussion about what has happened to employment during the recession leads naturally to a discussion about what can be expected for the recovery. Pew and Global Insight/U.S. Conference of Mayors estimate that currently, the green or clean energy economy includes over 750,000 jobs.[10] This section summarizes green economy-related job growth projections from three sources—PERI and the Center for American Progress, Global Insight (for the U.S. Conference of Mayors), and the President's Council of Economic Advisers (CEA). It is important to remember that each of these employment projections are estimates based on a specific set of assumptions and conditions; any of which could change as the economy transitions from recession to recovery.

As such, they are only intended as markers by which to measure future growth.

The green recovery program proposed by PERI and the Center for American Progress combines a $100 billion fiscal stimulus with an additional credit stimulus—through a federal loan guarantee program to boost private-sector investment in energy efficiency and renewable energy—to create 2 million jobs over two years.[11] Global Insight projects a similar number of jobs, but over a longer time horizon—2.5 million jobs by 2018, 3.5 million by 2028 and 4.2 million by 2038.[12] At the October 2009 levels of labor force participation and unemployment, the creation of 2 million jobs would bring the unemployment rate back to less than 9%.[13] If these jobs were distributed according to the current distribution of representative green occupations by race, the resulting rates of unemployment would be 8.4% for whites (compared to 9.5%); 14.9% for blacks (compared to 15.7%); 11.3% for Latinos (compared to 13.1%) and 6.2% for Asians (compared to 7.5%).[14]

Figure 6: *Change in Representative "Green" Job Labor Force by Race & Ethnicity*

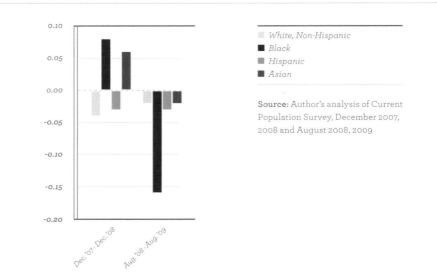

Legend:
- White, Non-Hispanic
- Black
- Hispanic
- Asian

Source: Author's analysis of Current Population Survey, December 2007, 2008 and August 2008, 2009

Using BLS Occupational Employment Projections, CEA projects 52% growth between 2000-2016 for a smaller category of "environment-related occupations,"[15] relative to a growth rate of 14% for all other occupations.[16] It is important to note that although the BLS projections do not reflect recent economic fluctuations, CEA reports that since ARRA investments to support "green" initiatives represent a boost to an industry that was already growing, ARRA should help to move the industry back toward its pre-recession growth path. Similarly, though not offered as a projection of future growth, Pew researchers report that between 1998 and 2007, the fastest rates of clean energy economy job growth occurred in the environmentally friendly production (67%) and clean energy (23%) sectors. Additionally, 83% of all venture capital investments made between 2006 and 2008 were made in these two sectors. Assuming this pattern of growth continues into the future, these sectors represent a range of jobs, including those related to solar- and wind-power generation (which dominate the clean energy category) and could have an impact on a wide range of existing industries—including transportation, manufacturing/industrial, construction, agriculture, energy production and materials—as demand for more environmentally friendly products continues to grow. In fact, most of the occupations listed in *Figure 1* are representative of the types of jobs critical to clean energy and environmentally-friendly production.

Next, we turn our discussion to the construction industry which has experienced more losses during this recession than any other industry.

However, given the high concentration of representative green occupations within this sector, it is also reasonable to expect that the construction industry would be positively affected by the transition to a green economy. This expectation is supported by revised industry projections released by the President's Council of Economic Advisers in July 2009 that indicate that for the period since the recession (2008-2016), construction industry jobs are projected to grow by more than 2 million jobs. This is up from the 780,000 jobs (2006-2016) originally projected by BLS. Again, the CEA attributes this to ARRA direct investments and incentives for private investment in infrastructure, the construction of power and communication structures and the weatherization of homes. Even with this more positive outlook, time is of the essence when it comes to investing in the green economy and creating much needed jobs. Based on CEA projections and holding all else constant, at the current pace of job losses in the construction industry (averaging -67,000 per month during the last six months), it would take only six more months to reduce the job growth potential implied by these projections to zero. In other words, two million jobs would only bring the construction industry back to its pre-recession level of employment.

Finally, while the construction industry as a whole stands to benefit greatly from a "green recovery," several other non-construction-related green jobs have been projected to experience large or fast growth over the next decade. Three representative green economy occupations are listed among BLS's 30 largest growth occupations for 2006-2016—computer software engineers, applications (# 15 and 226,000 jobs), truck drivers (# 20 and 193,000 jobs) and carpenters (# 23 and 150,000 jobs). Computer software engineers, with specialties in applications (#4 and 44.6% growth) and systems software (#25 and 28.2% growth), are also on the list of the 30 fastest growing occupations for 2006-2016.[17] Again, these projections were made prior to the start of the recession and should be referenced with caution.

Geographic Distribution of Green Jobs

Aside from the issue of when and how many green jobs will be created is the issue of where this growth will occur. While an important feature of most green economy jobs is that they tend to be domestic by nature (i.e. in the U.S. as opposed to abroad), it is also important to consider whether patterns of job growth and job placement will simply reinforce existing patterns of inequality or offer true mobility. Pew Charitable Trusts provides a state-by-state analysis of the current clean energy economy, including current jobs, businesses, job growth (1998-2007) and venture capital investments (2006-2008), in their report titled, *The Clean Energy Economy: Repowering Jobs, Businesses and Investments Across America*. Choosing to focus solely on producers and suppliers in the clean energy economy, they acknowledge that their analysis is conservative relative to others because they only count actual clean energy economy businesses and jobs rather than entire occupations (such as all jobs in mass transit, or all electricians). However, this narrower definition is referenced for this portion of the analysis because it provides a good framework for analyzing where growth can reasonably be expected to occur based on the current size

of an identifiable clean energy economy, and trends in job growth and private investment.

Figure 7, originally published in Pew (2009), categorizes states based on the size of their clean energy economy as well as the rate of growth in this industry from 1998 to 2007. States identified as having a "large" clean energy economy are those with more clean energy jobs than the national average of 15,106 jobs and those identified as "small" have less than the national average. Similarly, states with "fast growing" jobs are those with an annual job growth rate than exceeds the national average of 1.9%, those with "growing" industries are those with a positive rate of growth that was less than the national average, and those that are "losing" jobs have experienced negative growth. In August 2009, seven states with rates of unemployment that were significantly higher than the national average[18]—California, Florida, Michigan, North Carolina, Ohio, Oregon and Tennessee—also had large clean energy economies. Four high unemployment states—Nevada, Oregon, South Carolina and Tennessee—and the District of Columbia have fast growing clean energy economies. Five of the states with large or fast-growing clean energy economies—Illinois, Michigan, Ohio and South Carolina—and the District of Columbia also have rates of African American unemployment that exceed the national average (above 15% during the third quarter of 2009). This suggests that with timely and targeted investments in the green economy, including necessary investments in workforce development, the nation's transition to a green economy could have a significant impact on some of the most economically depressed areas of the country.

Figure 7: *Where are the Jobs in the Clean Energy Economy?*

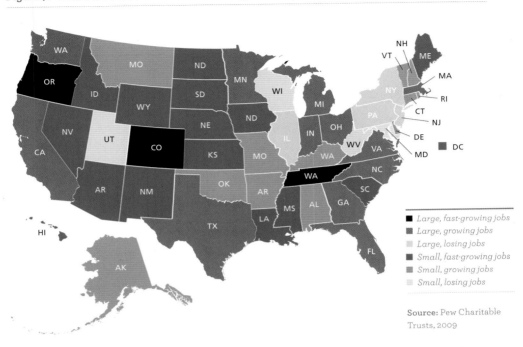

Legend:
- ■ *Large, fast-growing jobs*
- ■ *Large, growing jobs*
- ■ *Large, losing jobs*
- ■ *Small, fast-growing jobs*
- ■ *Small, growing jobs*
- ▦ *Small, losing jobs*

Source: Pew Charitable Trusts, 2009

While almost 6% of African American workers were in occupations that will be critical to building a green economy at the peak of the last economic expansion, the next logical question at this point is to what extent African Americans can expect to benefit from newly created jobs based on where these jobs are likely to be located. According to Pew's estimates regarding the clean energy economy, 72% of this country's total African-American population lives in a state with a large clean energy economy, while only 16% of all African Americans live in a state with a fast-growing clean energy economy.[19] Three states with fast-growing, albeit small, clean energy economies—Mississippi, South Carolina and Louisiana—and the District of Columbia have significant African-American populations (over 25% of the state's total population). Out of these, none are in the top ten for jobs in environmentally friendly production (the fastest growing segment of the clean energy economy between 1998 and 2007) and only the District of Columbia is in the top ten for jobs in clean energy (the second fastest growing segment). Furthermore, of these four areas, two (South Carolina and Louisiana) received no venture capital investments between 2006 and 2008. Therefore, the pattern of new investments and new job growth—be they predominantly in areas with an established green economy infrastructure or those with the most rapid growth—will prove to be a crucial element in the accessibility of these new jobs. As of November 6, 2009, less than one-tenth of ARRA funds available through the Department of Energy (total of $18.8 billion available) had been paid out.[20]

Policy Recommendations for Bringing Green Recovery to the Chronically Unemployed

Recognizing the dire need for jobs throughout the nation as a whole, and particularly in urban communities, the National Urban League has proposed a comprehensive *Plan for Putting Americans Back to Work* that includes a green jobs component as well as an accompanying workforce development plan. Specifically, this plan includes the creation of Green Empowerment Zones in areas where at least 50 percent of the population has an unemployment rate that is higher than the state average. Manufacturers of solar panels and wind turbines that open plants in high unemployment areas will for a period of three years, be eligible for a zero federal income tax rate and a zero capital gains tax under the condition that they hire and retain for a minimum of three years at least half of their workforce from the local area.

In response to critics who argue that the supply of labor in disadvantaged communities often lacks the skills necessary to obtain and maintain employment, NUL also proposes the creation of 100 Urban Jobs Academies to Implement an Expansion of the Urban Youth Empowerment Program (UYEP) to employ and train the chronically unemployed. UYEP, a four year demonstration project created in partnership with the U.S. Department of Labor in 2004, is a youth career preparation initiative designed for at-risk, out-of-school, and adjudicated youth and young adults between the ages of 18 and 24. With 27 Urban League affiliate sites and a total of $29.3 million, the program served 3,900 youth, 65 percent of whom either had job placements (paying an average wage of $9.32/hour) or completed their high school diploma or GED. Two hundred participants were placed in postsecondary schools or college upon completion of their secondary education. Scaling this program up to 100 sites would more than triple the program at a cost of $108.5 million.

In addition to these National Urban League recommendations, both the *Clean Energy Jobs and American Power Act,* introduced by Senators John Kerry (MA) and Barbara Boxer (CA), and the *American Clean Energy and Security Act* (ACES), passed by the House of Representatives in June, include two key provisions that could be beneficial for workers and communities that have been especially hard hit by the recession. *The Green Construction Careers Demonstration Project* creates middle class careers in the green economy for low-income Americans, and the *Funding the Green Jobs Act* helps train workers, particularly those from disadvantaged communities, for jobs in the clean energy economy.

Conclusion

While so-called green jobs will not be sufficient alone to bring this economy out of recession and spur the type of private job creation needed to fuel sustained economic growth, they will unquestionably be important in providing a foundation. As such, it is crucial that the National Urban League and other minority-serving community based organizations be at the forefront of preparing their constituents to participate in and reap the benefits of the emerging green economy, not only as employees, but also as business owners and employers. As this paper has demonstrated, this goal is well within reach, but will require diligence and persistence both in terms of securing available funding to provide needed training as well as staying informed of new developments and opportunities in this rapidly changing new segment of our economy.

REFERENCES

Apollo Alliance, Green for All, Center for American Progress and Center on Wisconsin Strategy. "Green Collar Jobs in America's Cities." 2008.

Bishop, John H. and Shani Carter. "How Accurate Are Recent BLS Occupational Projections?" Monthly Labor Review, 1991, 114(10): 37-43.

Center on Wisconsin Strategy, Workforce Alliance and Apollo Alliance. "Greener Pathways." 2008.

Council of Economic Advisers. "Preparing the Workers of Today for the Jobs of Tomorrow." Executive Office of the President, July 2009.

Global Insight for the United States Conference of Mayors and the Mayors Climate Protection Center.

"U.S. Metro Economies: Current and Potential Green Jobs in the U.S. Economy." 2008.

Hamilton, Darrick. "The Racial Composition of American Jobs." In The State of Black America 2006, edited by George E. Curry and Stephanie Jones, 77-115. New York: National Urban League, 2006.

Pew Charitable Trusts. "The Clean Energy Economy: Repowering Jobs, Businesses and Investments Across America." 2009.

Pollin, Robert, Heidi Garrett-Peltier, James Heintz and Helen Scharber. "Green Recovery: A Program to Create Good Jobs and Start Building a Low-Carbon Economy." Political Economy Research Institute and Center for American Progress, September 2008.

Pollin, Robert and Jeannette Wicks-Lim. "Job Opportunities for the Green Economy: A State by State Picture of Occupations that Gain from Green Investments." Political Economy Research Institute, University of Massachusetts, Amherst. June 2008.

Workforce Information Council Green Jobs Study Group. "Measurement and Analysis of Employment in the Green Economy." 2009.

NOTES

[1] When this analysis was done, the economy was in the 20th month of the recession that began in December 2007. The recession of the 1980s lasted 16 months from July 1981 to November 1982. These are the official dates reported by the Business Cycle Dating Committee of the National Bureau of Economic Research.

[2] Workforce Information Council Green Jobs Study Group (2009).

[3] Ibid

[4] Pollin and Wicks-Lim (2008); Center on Wisconsin Strategy, Workforce Alliance and Apollo Alliance (2008); Apollo Alliance, Green for All, Center for American Progress and Center on Wisconsin Strategy (2008).

[5] Pollin and Wicks-Lim (2008).

[6] Bureau of Labor Statistics, Occupational Employment Statistics, May 2008.

[7] Hamilton (2006).

[8] Bureau of Labor Statistics, Current Employment Statistics, December 2007 and August 2009 (preliminary).

[9] Bureau of Labor Statistics, Current Employment Statistics, August 2009 (preliminary).

[10] These estimates were obtained from private micro-level establishment data available in the NETS database that allows for identification of individual businesses by detailed industry sector.

[11] Pollin, et al (2008).

[12] These projections were made based upon a chosen set of assumptions regarding the share of electricity to be generated from alternative resources, the extent of retrofitting and the share of transportation fuels from renewable sources. See Global Insight (2008) for details.

[13] Author's calculations based on analysis of BLS's October 2009 Employment Situation report.

[14] Ibid

[15] The environment-related occupations considered included environmental engineering technicians, environmental engineers, environmental scientists and specialists (including health), and environmental science and protection technicians (including health).

[16] Council of Economic Advisers. (2009).

[17] Historically, BLS projections have tended to underestimate growth in higher skilled occupations while overestimating growth in lower skilled occupations. See Bishop and Carter (1991).

[18] Bureau of Labor Statistics, Local Area Unemployment Statistics, Regional and State Employment and Unemployment (Monthly), August 2009.

[19] The distribution of African-American workers in representative green economy occupations follows a similar pattern—70% in large green economy states and 17% in fast-growing states.

[20] Based on information from Recovery.gov accessed on November 23, 2009.

I. Lessons Learned from the Economic Crisis: Job Creation & Economic Recovery

BERNARD E. ANDERSON, PH.D.

In late 2009, the American economy appeared to begin recovery from the worst economic crisis since the Great Depression. The National Bureau of Economic Research marked December 2007 as the beginning of the recession and over the next 22 months, the economy lost more than eight million jobs. The employment contraction spread widely across the economy with almost all industries reporting job losses at some time over the 23 month period. Health care, the only industry reporting job gains throughout the recession, gained nearly 600,000 jobs since 2007. The rate of unemployment was 10.0 percent in December 2009 and the number of unemployed was 15.3 million; 38.6 percent had been jobless for more than six months.

Reflecting the long, persistent racial disparity in the labor market, the black unemployment rate was 15.6 percent, or 1.6 times that among white workers. Black workers were 13.9 percent of the labor force, 12.9 percent of the employed, but almost twice that ratio—22.1 percent—of the unemployed. Black youth ages 16-19 were unemployed at 45.7 percent, or 1.8 times that of similarly aged white youth.

The depth and breadth of job losses during the recession was the result of the dual onslaught of economic contraction and the collapse of the financial system. Starting in fall 2008, banks faced a severe liquidity crisis which forced them to suspend credit for consumers and for small and large businesses. More than 100 banks failed while bank regulatory authorities forced others to strengthen their capital and tighten underwriting standards. Even credit-worthy

borrowers found it difficult to obtain credit for inventory and cash flow management. The financial crisis generated reduced consumer spending and business investment, spurring an across the board surge in layoffs.

Getting America Back to Work

In February 2009, the Obama administration proposed, and Congress enacted, the American Recovery and Reinvestment Act of 2009. The $787 billion stimulus program included funding for extended unemployment compensation, middle class tax cuts to bolster consumer demand, tax incentives for business investment, aid to state and local governments, funding for infrastructure, and job training for occupations in the health care, energy and environmental sectors. The U.S. Department of Labor received $700 million to support job training initiatives in those industries. Though the stimulus program has had its detractors, the Congressional Budget Office estimates that the

Figure 1: Unemployment Rate During Last Three Recessions*

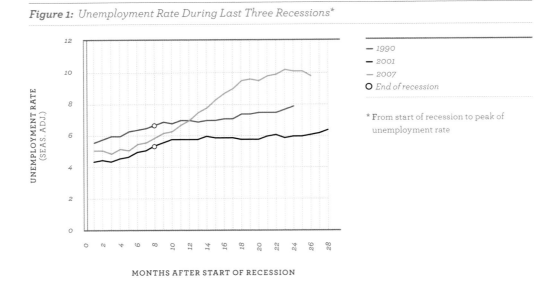

stimulus program might have been responsible for saving or creating about 1.2 million jobs.

The Path to Recovery

Despite many efforts to spur economic recovery, the labor market remains weak and many economists question the prospects for rapid recovery in the immediate months ahead. In the past, a short, deep decline in employment was followed by rapid job growth during the recovery (a V-shaped recovery) while a slow, shallow decline in jobs was followed by a long, jobless recovery (a U-shaped recovery). In a jobless recovery, the unemployment rate remains high long after recovery begins. As *Figure 1* shows, during the 8 month 1990-91 recession, employment declined by nearly 2.0 percent and the unemployment rate climbed to 6.8 percent by the end of the recession. But, joblessness kept rising during the 1992 recovery and reached a peak of 7.8 percent in June 1992, 15 months after the recession ended. Similarly, during the eight months of the 2001 recession, the unemployment rate rose to 5.5 percent, but more than a year and a half after that, it topped out at 6.3 percent.

The unemployment rate remains high during a weak recovery because with a glimmer of hope that jobs might be available, workers who dropped out of the labor force will return. The increase in the size of the labor force is likely to exceed the rate of job creation, thereby contributing to a continuing high rate of unemployment.

There is reason to believe job creation will be modest during the extant recovery and that unemployment might remain high for an extended length of time. The consensus among economists is that gross domestic product (GDP) growth will be in the neighborhood of 2.0 - 2.5 percent through 2010. At that rate, the economy might not reach full employment, measured at 5.5 percent, until well into 2013 or later. More than 10 million jobs are needed to satisfy the natural growth of the working age population (now about 2.0 percent) and to re-employ those who lost jobs during the long 2007-09 recession.

The job creation challenge is exacerbated by two forces at work in the American economy—structural change and cyclical fluctuation. The labor market response to cyclical fluctuation is driven by the pattern of employer adjustment to the demand for labor. In a period of modest growth, employers satisfy additional demand for labor by first increasing hours of work and then by hiring temporary workers. Employers hire full-time workers only when confident of sustained recovery and future growth.

Historical Redux

Structural change in the labor market can be traced to development over the past century. From the late 19th through the mid-20th century, job growth in the American labor market was concentrated in basic industries like autos, steel and glass, as well as in transportation and utilities. Manufacturing was king as increasingly large corporations expanded production to satisfy growing consumer demand. The secular trend in employment growth was interrupted by the Great Depression, and side tracked by World War II (WW II), when domestic production gave way to defense production. Domestic production resumed after the war as corporations converted back to household products. The pent up demand for consumer goods and services, housing and other products generated a strong increase in output across industries and a surge in employment across the board.

The U.S. emerged from WW II as the world's leading industrial power. That created opportunities not only for high levels of domestic production, but also for export. The demand for labor was robust and jobs were plentiful for the growing American labor force. The average rate of unemployment between 1948 and 1954 was 4.6 percent and was less than 4.0 percent in 4 of the 6 years.

During the 1950s, the American economy began to change in ways that loosened the relationship between economic growth and job creation. Technological change introduced a new paradigm in the industrial sector. New forms of business organization evolved as did new methods for managing employees. The technological advancements in production, mainly automation, were biased toward less labor input per unit of output. New methods for human resource management changed employer/employee relations in ways that reduced labor turnover, improved labor productivity, and restrained new hiring. Job creation and employment steadily moved toward concentration in small and mid-sized firms, especially new businesses in emerging industries.

The transformation of the American economy over the past four decades was most evident in the growth of the services sector. Health services, telecommunications, financial services and education emerged as major contributors to GDP and employment. Today, they remain key sectors for job growth as the

economy emerges from the 2007-09 recession. Biotechnology, nanotechnology, energy and the environment are also expected to be growth sectors.

Outsourcing is another feature of the contemporary labor market that will affect domestic job creation as the economy recovers. Estimates of outsourcing—the relocation of domestic jobs to other countries—vary widely, ranging from the AFL-CIO's estimate of 2 million jobs, to the National Association of Manufacturer's 300,000 jobs. The real number, no doubt, lies in between. But whatever the correct number, outsourcing reduces the number of new jobs that otherwise might be available to American workers as business conditions improve.

Over time, outsourcing has spread across a wide range of industries from manufacturing to services and from low value-added to high wage occupations. With the diffusion of fiber optic technology, outsourcing is now used widely in customer service communication, medical diagnosis, engineering and research and development. On the other hand, some jobs may be classified as "insourcing"—jobs held by American workers employed by U.S. based foreign companies. The number of net new jobs created from such export-import transactions is difficult to estimate but must be considered when projecting job creation during economic recovery.

The relationship between production and •unemployment is expressed in Okun's Law. This relationship, codified by Arthur Okun, a distinguished economist and former Chairman of the President's Council of

Economic Advisors during the 1960s, is based on an analysis of aggregate production and employment variables. Simply stated, for every 3.0 percent increase in output, there is a 1.0 percent decline in the unemployment rate, a 5.0 percent increase in the labor force, and a 1.0 percent increase in productivity. In the current economic cycle, however, the relationship might be altered by a change in the number of discouraged workers or worker productivity. The diffusion of computer technology might have also altered the long term stability in Okun's Law, so that today, fewer new jobs are created for each percentage point increase in output. But, because the labor force participation rate has remained in the neighborhood of 65 percent over a long period of time, the decline in the labor/output ratio is likely explained mainly by an increase in labor productivity.

> Outsourcing reduces the number of new jobs that otherwise might be available to American workers.

Policy Options for Job Creation
Concerned that economic recovery might be weak and unstable, the Obama administration and Congress have proposed new initiatives to spur employment growth. The policy menu includes tax incentives for small businesses, targeted employment tax credits, public employment through aid to state and local government, and direct job creation. These and other measures were included in a jobs bill that was introduced by the Congressional Black Caucus (CBC) late last year. Among other measures, the CBC bill also included support for 100,000 jobs through direct grants to community based organizations.

Such initiatives are based on the proven model of direct job creation that was implemented during recovery from the 1974-75 recession. At that time, grants made to the National Urban League and other community based organizations provided job training and employment assistance to thousands of disadvantaged youth and young adults in urban areas. Similar measures are necessary at this time to address the unprecedented joblessness generated by the recent economic crisis which exacerbated the already weak labor market conditions existing in many communities before the recession began.

The invisible hand of the market will not produce full employment. It never has, and it never will. Carefully crafted public policy is necessary to help restore full employment and a sine qua non for reducing racial inequality in the labor market.

II. Creating Good Jobs for Everyone

LABOR SECRETARY HILDA L. SOLIS

When I took leadership of the Department of Labor in February 2009, the African-American unemployment rate had already risen approximately 75 percent; going from 7.7 percent in August 2007 to an astounding 13.5 percent. This downturn occurred after an economic expansion that failed to generate jobs, did not increase incomes and raised poverty levels. Workers were (and are still) struggling to feed their families, pay bills, and plan for retirement as unemployment levels were reaching highs that we had not seen in decades. We acted quickly to assist workers and their families in light of devastating job losses and the Administration and I remain committed to lowering the unemployment rates for all individuals. Still, we are deeply concerned about obstacles facing certain communities.

African Americans in Past and Current Labor Markets

It is important to view the current situation for African Americans from a long-term perspective in order to understand the full scope of the problem. Historically, African-American workers have faced great disadvantages in the labor market. Even when the economy was doing well in the 1990s, African Americans were 2.2 times more likely to be unemployed than whites. However, since President Obama took office, African Americans on average have been 1.8 times more likely to be unemployed compared to whites; this is an historic low. From 1972 to 2009, the ratio of unemployment rates for African Americans relative to Whites was an average of 2.2.

For the eight years of this century before President Obama took office, African Americans had only a small window where the unemployment rate was declining. However, compared to the labor market conditions experienced by white workers, the African American unemployment situation was worse during that period than now. From 2000 to 2008, the ratio of unemployment rates for African Americans relative to whites averaged 2.1.

Compared to previous recessions, African Americans also seem to be doing relatively better in this recession. While the recent 16.5 percent unemployment rate for African Americans is the highest for any racial or ethnic group, it is still below the unemployment rate faced by African Americans during the last severe recession. The last time the unemployment rate for whites was higher than 9 percent was in March 1983, and at that time, the African-American unemployment rate was 20.1 percent. If the historical 2.2 ratio of unemployment rates were to hold, we could expect that African Americans would face an unemployment rate of 19.1 percent (8.7 unemployment rate for White multiplied by 2.2.) instead of 16.5 percent.

While it is not acceptable that African Americans remain disproportionately more likely to be unemployed, the disadvantages faced by African Americans today are no doubt a continuation of a weak labor market at the beginning of this century. The challenge of job recovery will involve addressing both the structural and cyclical components of unemployment.

Understanding the Movement of the African American Unemployment Rate

There are two policy challenges when it comes to addressing the African American unemployment rate. First, there are some workers who always had higher unemployment rates because they lacked competitive skills (this can be seen as a structural issue). Second, there are some workers who were impacted by the current job loss wave although they had jobs and were job ready (this is described as a cyclical issue). Clearly, with the African American unemployment rate increase from 8 to 16.5 percent in the last three years, it cannot be the case that the structural unemployment problem should be used to characterize the only source of unemployment in the African American community.

Unemployment levels have gone up for white and African Americans of all education levels since 2007. However, the unemployment rates for African Americans with less than a high school diploma relative to White dropouts have been roughly the same throughout this downturn, going from an African American-to-white ratio of 1.51 in January 2007 to 1.53 in 2010. But, African Americans with college degrees have seen their unemployment rate increase relative to White college graduates from a ratio of 1.19 in January 2007 to 1.96 in January 2010. If we think of those with less education as facing long-term structural unemployment problems, and those with higher education and lower unemployment rates as facing cyclical unemployment, these data help highlight the need to address job loss caused by this downturn in the African American community.

It is important that we respond with programs that recognize the large cyclical component of African American unemployment. We must take steps to get those facing cyclical unemployment retrained and back into the labor market so that the length of their unemployment does not become a permanent impediment and result in increasing the number of workers who are structurally unemployed.

"Good Jobs for Everyone"

Since I became Secretary of Labor, I have made it a priority for the Department to ensure that historically underserved communities are not left behind as we recover from the recession. We can and will do better to increase the number of employed African Americans. My vision for the Department is *Good Jobs for Everyone*. I am proud of all the Department has accomplished under the American Reinvestment and Recovery Act (Recovery Act), and my vision of *Good Jobs for Everyone*

is being implemented in all Recovery Act projects that the Department has engaged in.

Here are some of the ways that I define a good job.

» *A good job can support a family by increasing incomes, narrowing the wage gap (for example, wage gaps between men and women and gaps experienced by communities of color), and allowing workplace flexibility.*

» *A good job is safe and secure and gives people a voice in the workplace.*

» *A good job is sustainable and innovative, for example a green job.*

» *A good job will help rebuild a strong middle class.*

» *A good job provides access to a secure retirement and to adequate and affordable health coverage.*

This economic downturn has not created the same disadvantages for African Americans experienced in the 1980 downturns with respect to relative unemployment rates, or disadvantages in employment. This is due in part to the Recovery Act. The Recovery Act delivered help to people in the form of expanded unemployment benefits and a large tax cut aimed at working Americans. By strengthening the safety-net, putting money directly in the pockets of Americans, and supporting state and local governments to maintain the services that working families rely on. The Recovery Act helped sustain neighborhoods ravaged by job losses so that the harm to neighborhood-level economies was not as severe as in the 1980s.

We also increased investments in training, so that we can build a more inclusive recovery. The roles of the Department of Labor have been to help shore up the safety-net for people who have been knocked down by the economy and to build a path forward for people as we recover.

The actions that the Department has taken under the Recovery Act have put people back to work and have saved jobs. We have worked hard to ensure that African American communities are benefitting from the Recovery Act. I have visited numerous Recovery Act-funded projects in communities across the country. Over $55 billion has been provided to states to support and expand Unemployment Insurance (UI), and more than $3 billion has been issued in grants to states to provide training and employment services to adults, dislocated workers and youth. We acted quickly to protect workers who lost their jobs and provide new training opportunities for them and for people looking to upgrade their skills or change careers.

We worked with states to make changes to eligibility requirements for UI benefits, giving more jobless workers access to benefits, and extended the period of eligibility for workers who lost their jobs. We also quickly increased the amount of unemployment benefits that people received by $25 a week. This money is especially helpful in areas where urban communities have to struggle with high cost-of-living expenses.

The Department is also looking for innovative ways to promote economic recovery. For example, employment training services are divided by geographic boundaries even though regional economies cross city and state lines. That is why we created the Regional Economic Impact National Emergency Grant (NEG), which allows for a regional approach to workforce services. Several states impacted

by automotive layoffs, such as Michigan, have received funding through this mechanism. The Department provided a NEG of $18.6 million to assist over 1,000 workers affected by layoffs in Southeast Michigan, which includes several counties and the Detroit Metropolitan Area.

During my travels throughout the country, I have met people who have gone back to school and changed careers to prepare themselves for 21st Century jobs. Jobs continue to grow in the clean energy and health care sectors. Green jobs play an important role in our economic recovery, and like so many other jobs in the construction trades, they tend to pay above average wages. The President and I believe that they are the jobs of the future.

The Department has invested $750 million for worker training and placement programs to prepare workers for careers in high growth and emerging industries. This includes $500 million for research, labor exchange, and job training projects in the energy efficiency and renewable energy industries.

Several of our Green Capacity Building Grants were awarded to programs that train our nation's youth. For example, the Department awarded the Urban League of Broward County with $100,000 to expand its YouthBuild programs to include a green building and green careers capacity building component. The Springfield Urban League was awarded $100,000 to develop an initiative to ensure that YouthBuild participants in Illinois and communities of color have the necessary resources to access opportunities in the growing clean energy economy. Similarly, the Tri-County Urban League partnered with the City of Peoria Workforce Development Department and others to strengthen the current YouthBuild Peoria project by providing participants with green building trades/ construction skills through enhanced union apprenticeship programs. The program will also connect youth to a new associate degree program in green construction. This project also received $100,000 from the Department.

The roles of the Department of Labor have been to help shore up the safety-net for people who have been knocked down by the economy and to build a path forward for people as we recover.

With the aging of our population and other factors, the demand for health care workers continues to grow rapidly. Hospitals and other ambulatory care settings, such as long-term care facilities, added approximately 25,000 new jobs in February 2009 even though 681,000 jobs across the nation were eliminated that month. The Bureau of Labor Statistics projects that health care and social assistance employers will generate four million new jobs between 2008

and 2018. It is likely that African Americans will benefit from the job growth. In 2008, there were about 4.5 million African Americans—more than one in four employed African Americans— working in education and health services. To help meet demand in these growing sectors, the Department awarded $220 million in Recovery Act grants to assist workers pursue careers in health care and other high growth and emerging industry sectors.

In creating the criteria for many of the grants funded by the Recovery Act, we required applicants to include partners made up of a diverse set of stakeholders, including labor organizations, public or private employers, and the local workforce system. We also gave special consideration for partnerships that included community-based organizations. We made it a priority to award grants to applicants who serve low-income workers, unemployed youth and adults, high school dropouts, communities of color, areas of high poverty, and other underserved sectors and vulnerable members of the workforce. We also set aside funding to serve workers who were hardest hit by the restructuring of the automotive industry.

And in our efforts to train workers, we created new partnerships with other departments, such as the U.S. Department of Housing and Urban Development, so that we connect residents in public housing with green jobs. In a joint letter, Secretary Donovan and I encouraged local Workforce Investment Boards and Public Housing Agencies to work together to bolster pathways to training and employment for residents of HUD housing.

We know returning veterans can contribute greatly to our economy. The Veterans' Employment and Training Service (VETS) is actively working to provide services to homeless veterans, with an increased emphasis on assisting homeless women veterans, whose numbers have increased. More than 7,000 African-American veterans are being served through the Department's Homeless Veterans Reintegration Program. VETS is also vigilant in assuring veterans' rights to reemployment after returning from a deployment to fight for our country are protected.

I also know that our youth face employment challenges. In July 2009, the unemployment rate for African-American youth ages 16 to 24 was 31.2 percent. The Recovery Act also provided funding to local areas to support programs that employed 317,584 youth this past summer. Recovery Act funding supported real work opportunities for our nation's youth in a variety of industries including green and other high growth and emerging industries. These jobs provided critical early labor market experience for youth, an experience which will increase their long-run labor market success. Of the youth who participated in our summer youth programs, approximately 45 percent were African American, 39 percent were White, and 24 percent were Latino.

This is a tumultuous and challenging time for urban communities, but we have already made a real difference in the lives of America's workers and their families. We successfully implemented the Recovery Act and have seen how these investments have saved and created jobs in communities across the country. Looking forward, the Department of Labor will continue to work hard to ensure that there are *Good Jobs for Everyone* and to ensure that all communities, particularly those that have historically been underserved, are included in our recovering economy.

III. Housing in the Post-Bubble Economy

LANCE FREEMAN, PH.D.

Housing is fundamental to human survival and well being; second perhaps only to food in material importance. Housing provides shelter, and for most people, is the place where more time is spent than any other. For American homeowners, it also happens to be the primary store of wealth. Consequently, housing impacts not only material well-being but life chances as well. In setting the goal of ensuring that every American lives in safe, decent, affordable and energy efficient housing on fair terms by the year 2025, the National Urban League seeks to do its part to create a society where fundamental needs and life chances are not conditioned on circumstances or location of birth.

This report shows that although access to safe and decent housing as a reality for every black American seems within our grasp, affordability, energy efficiency and fairness remain a distant lodestar that will require Herculean efforts to achieve by 2025. Furthermore, the housing bubble-induced economic downturn and jobs crisis threaten to postpone and even reverse the progress made towards achieving the goal. This chapter highlights the current state of black America on the various dimensions of the goal, assesses the impact of the economic downturn and concludes by outlining several steps that would likely increase the prospects of achieving this laudable goal.

Affordable Housing on Fair Terms

The current economic downturn that began in December 2007 was spawned, in part, by the lack of access to housing finance on fair terms as many households were misled into taking on mortgages they could not afford. These bad loans went on to become toxic assets that threatened the solvency of numerous financial institutions, led to a curtailment of lending and investing, erosion in confidence and ultimately a collapsing economy. The fallout from the collapse of the housing market has been severe and blacks have borne much of the brunt of the economic downturn.

The most visible signs of fallout have been foreclosures and unemployment. Already some 1.5 million homes have been lost to foreclosure and by the end of 2009, the national unemployment rate was 10% while the black unemployment rate was over 16%.[1] Although racial breakdowns of foreclosure data are not available, we do know that blacks are overrepresented among those with subprime loans—the type of loan most likely to be in default.[2] Foreclosures, of course, are but the end result of financial distress. For many households this distress stems from onerous mortgage terms that would have been difficult to meet in the best of times. However, over the course of the recession, mounting job losses have pushed

---

Figure 1: *Rent Burdens*

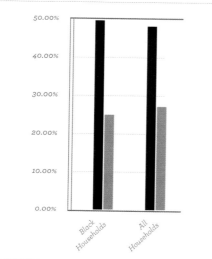

■ *Moderate Rent Burden*
■ *Severe Rent Burden*

Source: Author's tabulation of 2008 American Community Survey

otherwise secure homeowners into financial distress. A reduction in income, whether due to unemployment or lower wages, translates into less income with which to pay for housing costs and consequently, higher housing cost burdens. This is a problem that afflicts both owners and renters alike.

Figure 1 illustrates the percentage of black Americans and non-black Americans with moderate incomes who have moderate or severe rent burdens. Moderate income households are those earning less than 120% of the median income in the household's respective metropolitan area. The household has a moderate housing cost burden if they expend more than 30% of their income on housing costs and a severe housing cost burden if they spend more than 50% of their income on housing costs. As a general rule of thumb, moderate income households spending more than 30% of income for housing are said to be in a financially precarious position.[3]

According to *Figure 1*, housing affordability is a prevalent problem for moderate income renters. Half of all moderate income black renter households pay more than 30% of their incomes for rent and nearly one in four moderate income black renter households pay more than half of their incomes for rent. If we consider rent burdens for the entire population, the picture improves only slightly. Forty-three percent of all black renter households have a moderate rent burden and 23% of all black renter households have a severe rent burden (these figures are not presented in *Figure 1*).

The affordability problem appears to be even more dire when we consider the cost burdens among moderate income owners as depicted in *Figure 2*. Nearly 60% of moderate income black households that are owners pay more than 30% of their incomes for housing costs and 31% of this group pay more than half their incomes for housing costs. Among blacks, moderate income owners actually appear to be in more

Figure 2: *Housing Cost Burdens for Owners*

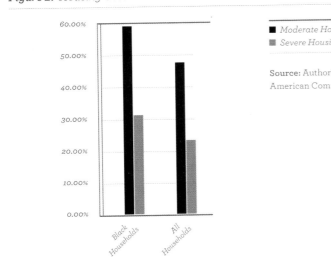

■ *Moderate Housing Cost Burden*
■ *Severe Housing Cost Burden*

Source: Author's tabulation of 2008 American Community Survey

precarious straits than moderate income renters. In fact, although homeownership is typically associated with increased security, for moderate income blacks, homeowners actually appear to be less secure in the sense that they have proportionately less income available to cover other expenses. Interestingly, this pattern is not repeated for non-black Americans. While moderate and severe cost burdens are prevalent among home owning non-blacks with moderate incomes, the prevalence of such burdens is not appreciably higher than that found among non-black renters with moderate incomes. However, because the security associated with homeownership is turned upside down for many moderate income blacks, the implications of this economic downturn, sparked in part by unsound lending practices, will likely worsen the rent and housing cost burdens depicted in *Figures 1 and 2*, respectively, as renters and owners alike find housing costs consuming a growing share of their declining incomes.

The greater precariousness associated with homeownership for moderate income blacks is suggestive of the obstacles that remain in achieving the goal of access to housing "on fair terms." In fact, black Americans have routinely been denied access to housing, except in segregated neighborhoods, and excluded from commercial housing finance markets.[4] Although discrimination in housing markets may have declined in the latter half of the 20th century, at the turn of the century nearly one in five would be renters or homeowners could expect to face discriminatory treatment if they were black (Turner 2002). Studies that tested whether blacks are treated differently in lending markets found a similar result and a significant proportion of

blacks are likely to encounter discriminatory treatment when seeking a mortgage.[5] Moreover, many subprime borrowers have been found to have credit profiles that would qualify them for prime rate loans, adding credibility to allegations of borrowers being taken advantage of by unscrupulous financial institutions.[6] One result is the finding described in the previous paragraph, whereby moderate income black homeowners find themselves in more precarious straits than otherwise similar renters. Thus, there is ample reason to suspect that there is still work to do to ensure that everyone has access to housing on fair terms.

But, if there is one silver lining associated with the economic downturn, it may be in the public outrage over the abuses and predatory actions of some lenders and brokers that has pushed some policymakers to attempt to rein in the most abusive and deceptive practices in the mortgage market. If policies such as the creation of a Consumer Financial Protection Agency are adopted, it's less likely borrowers will wind up with mortgages that have unfair terms.

Access to Safe and Decent Housing

Safe and decent housing has been the aim of reformers since the progressive movement of the late 19th century. As newer housing that met building codes was developed and older housing was retired, the quality of the housing stock gradually improved over the ensuing decades. The urban renewal program of the middle 20th century further eradicated much substandard housing. This program made federal funds available to local governments to demolish "slum" housing ostensibly to be replaced with newer but still affordable

Figure 3: *Housing Quality*

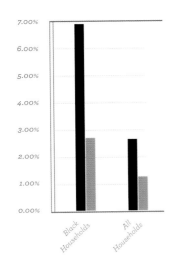

Legend:
- ■ *Moderately Inadequate*
- ■ *Severely Inadequate*

Source: Author's tabulation of 2007 American Housing Survey

housing. Although urban renewal fell short in the development of newer affordable housing, it did accelerate the destruction of millions of substandard housing units. Finally, rising incomes also contributed to the demise of much substandard housing. As the US grew richer, even many poor households had the means to acquire housing that was decent and safe.

Figure 3 illustrates housing quality for American households as of 2007, the latest year for which data is available. Reflecting rising living standards and urban renewal programs that demolished much substandard housing, *Figure 3* shows that only a small portion of Americans have inadequate housing in a physical sense.[7] Approximately 7% of black Americans live in housing that is moderately inadequate and another 3% live in housing that is severely inadequate; making black Americans about twice as likely as other Americans to live in either moderate or severely inadequate housing.

Unfortunately, while the vast majority of black Americans have already achieved the goal of living in safe and decent housing, there remain more than 360,000 black households living in substandard housing conditions.

In addition to the assessment of housing "adequacy," overcrowding—typically defined by housing analysts as more than one person per room—must also be considered when assessing whether black Americans have access to safe and decent housing. Overcrowding has been one way that households of modest means have been able to obtain safe and decent housing. For example, a family without the means to secure safe and decent housing on their own might move in with another family that has access to such housing. Although this may be a viable solution to the access problem, some studies have linked overcrowding to higher rates of mortality and juvenile

Figure 4: *Crowding Conditions*

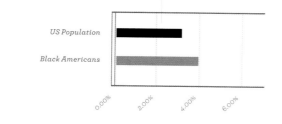

Source: Author's tabulation of 2008 American Community Survey

delinquency and symptoms of anxiety and depression among adults.[8]

Figure 4 illustrates overcrowding rates as of 2008 for all Americans and black Americans, respectively. Although the overwhelming majority of Americans—both black and non-black—do not live in crowded conditions, blacks are somewhat more likely to live in an overcrowded unit than non-blacks. This difference may be reflective of lower average incomes among blacks; yet, even among blacks, the overcrowding rate does not quite reach four percent.

Although *Figures 3 and 4* do not depict housing inadequacy and overcrowding as widespread problems, the jobs crisis could potentially have negative implications for the overall incidence of these housing conditions. Where poor housing conditions persist, they do so in part because of lax building regulations that allow landlords and owners to under maintain their properties, but also because there are households with limited means who cannot afford to move out of a dilapidated rental unit or to properly maintain an owner-occupied property. The higher unemployment, declining wages and lost wealth stemming from the economic downturn have served to increase the pool of households facing greater restrictions on their finances. For renters, this limits the

ability to be more selective about their place of residence. For owners, this means less money available for property maintenance—both in terms of the physical structure and financial obligations to the lender. Without appropriate interventions, the wave of foreclosures stemming from the housing bust will only serve to worsen the quality of housing stock as many foreclosed properties sit empty and deteriorate, dragging down surrounding property values.[9]

The Quest for Energy Efficient Housing
Although precise estimates of how many black Americans are currently living in energy efficient homes is not available, we can assume that even with the incentives for energy efficient retrofitting made available to households through the American Recovery and Reinvestment Act (ARRA), the jobs crisis has made the achievement of every black American living in energy efficient housing that much more difficult. This is because there is typically some increased initial outlay associated with retrofitting an existing home to meet energy efficiency standards and new energy efficient houses sell for a premium.[10] For cash strapped households or those uncertain about job security, this additional marginal cost may be enough to forego upgrading their home for

energy efficiency. Moreover, the construction of new housing, which tends to be more energy efficient, has been sharply curtailed during the economic slump. Newer energy efficient housing therefore comprises a smaller share of the housing stock than would have otherwise been the case. Overall, the economic downturn likely makes the achievement of energy efficiency in all homes a more distant reality.

Achieving the Goal

This chapter makes clear that the biggest housing problem for black Americans is not so much a housing problem but an income problem. Too many black Americans spend an undue amount of their income for housing and given, the current state of the labor market, housing cost burdens are a growing problem among households. Addressing this problem is fairly straightforward but it will cost money and require political will. The easiest way to address the problem of affordability would be to provide additional housing assistance to low- and moderate-income households that currently spend an undue portion of their incomes on housing. There are numerous ways of doing this. An obvious first step would be expanding access to the Housing Choice Voucher (HCV) program. The HCV pays the difference between what a household can afford and the Fair Market rent. Programs that produce affordable housing, such as the Low Income Housing Tax Credit, could be expanded as well. By increasing the supply of affordable housing, fewer households would have to spend inordinate amounts of their income on housing.

Housing assistance to low- and moderate-income households can even serve the objective of energy efficiency. As described in the previous section, energy efficiency typically requires some upfront expense that may deter some households from either moving into an energy efficient unit or upgrading their current unit. But with housing assistance, newer and more energy efficient housing is more likely to be within the reach of even low and moderate income households. Furthermore, the quest to retrofit housing units for energy efficiency, particularly in low- to moderate-income communities, serves as an important channel for job creation in these neighborhoods.

> ...with housing assistance, newer and more energy efficient housing is more likely to be within the reach of even low and moderate income households.

Ensuring that everyone has access to housing on fair terms, however, will require more than increasing housing assistance. The creation of a Consumer Financial Protection Agency would offer more protection to would be borrowers. But strengthening the enforcement of existing fair lending laws is also needed. Black Americans suffered disproportionately in the marketing of predatory loan products, but disparate treatment based on race, though illegal, is difficult to prove. Paired audits have been shown to be effective tools for detecting discrimination.[11] Devoting more resources for conducting such audits could be a fruitful way of ferreting out mortgage discrimination and ultimately deterring it in the future. Strengthening the enforcement of fair housing laws and utilizing audits to deter housing discrimination would also likely improve housing conditions for black Americans.

Despite the setbacks brought about by the recession and ensuing jobs crisis, each of these steps would likely contribute to measurable progress on the goal of ensuring that every American lives in safe, decent, affordable and energy efficient housing on fair terms.

REFERENCES

Courchane, M., Brian J. Surette and Peter M. Zorn. (2004). "Subprime Borrowers: Mortgage Transitions and Outcomes." *Journal of Real Estate Finance and Economics*, 29(4): 365-392.

Greening, L. A., David L. Greene, Carmen Difiglio (2008). "Energy efficiency and consumption—the rebound effect—a survey." *Energy Policy* 28: 389-401.

Immergluck, D. (2009). *Foreclosed*. Ithaca, NY, Cornell University Press.

Lending, C. f. R. (2009). "Snapshot of a Foreclosure Crisis." Retrieved January 21, 2010, 2009, from *http://www.responsiblelending.org/mortgage-lending/research-analysis/snapshot-of-a-foreclosure-crisis.html*.

Lepore, S. (1998). Encyclopedia of Housing. *The Encyclopedia of Housing*. W. v. Vliet. Thousand Oaks, CA, Sage Publications: 99-102.

Massey, D. S. and N. A. Denton (1993). *American apartheid : segregation and the making of the underclass*. Cambridge, Mass., Harvard University Press.

Plunz, R. (1990). *A History of Housing in New York City*. New York, Columbia University Press.

Schwartz, A. F. (2006). Housing Policy In the United States. New York, Routledge.

Turner, M. A., Fred Freiberg, Erin B. Godfrey, Carla Herbig, Diane K. Levy, Robin E. Smith (2002). All Other Things Being Equal: A Paired Testing Study of Mortgage Lending Institutions. Washington, D.C., Urban Institute.

Turner, M. A., Stephen L. Ross, George Galster, John Yinger (2002). Discrimination in Metropolitan Housing Markets National Results from Phase I of HDS2000. Washington, D.C., Urban Institute.

NOTES

[1] Center for Responsible Lending, "Snapshot of a Foreclosure Crisis." Retrieved January 21, 2010, 2009, from *http://www.responsiblelending.org/mortgage-lending/research-analysis/snapshot-of-a-foreclosure-crisis.html*

[2] Jones, Stephanie, "The Subprime Meltdown, Disarming the 'Weapons of Mass Deception,'" *The State of Black America 2009: Message to the President*, National Urban League (2009), pp. 157-164.

[3] Schwartz, A.F., Housing Policy in the United States, Routledge (2006).

[4] Massey, D.S. and N.A. Denton, *American Apartheid: Segregation and the Making of the Underclass*, Harvard University Press (1993).

[5] Turner, M. A., Fred Freiberg, Erin B. Godfrey, Carla Herbig, Diane K. Levy, Robin E. Smith, *All Other Things Being Equal: A Paired Testing Study of Mortgage Lending Institutions*, Urban Institute (2002); Turner, M. A., Stephen L. Ross, George Galster, John Yinger, *Discrimination in Metropolitan Housing Markets National Results from Phase I of HDS2000*, Urban Institute (2002).

[6] Courchane, M., Brian J. Surette and Peter M. Zorn, "Subprime Borrowers: Mortgage Transitions and Outcomes," *Journal of Real Estate Finance and Economics* (2004), 29(4): 365-392.

[7] A unit is considered severely inadequate if it has less than 2 full bathrooms and the unit has at least one of the following:

1. Unit does not have hot and cold running water

2. Unit does not have a bathtub or shower

3. Unit does not have a flush toilet

4. Unit shares plumbing facilities

5. Unit was cold for 24 hours or more and there have been more than 2 breakdowns of the heating equipment that lasted longer than 6 hours

6. Electricity is not used

7. Unit has exposed wiring and not every room has working electrical plugs and the fuses have blown more than twice

OR the unit has at least five of the following problems.

8. Unit has had outside water leaks in the last 12 months

9. Unit has had inside water leaks in the last 12 months

10. Unit has holes in the floor

11. Unit has open cracks wider than a dime

12. Unit has an area of peeling paint larger than 8 x 11

13. Rats have been seen recently in the unit

A unit is considered moderately inadequate if at least three problem among items 8-13 or it meets one of the following conditions:

14. There have been more than 2 breakdowns of the toilet that lasted longer than 6 hours

15. The main heating equipment is unvented room heaters burning kerosene, gas, or oil

16. The unit is lacking complete kitchen facilities

[8] Lepore, S., *The Encyclopedia of Housing*. W. v. Vliet. Thousand Oaks, CA, Sage Publications: 99-102.

[9] Immergluck, D., *Foreclosed*, Cornell University Press (2009).

[10] Greening, L. A., David L. Greene, Carmen Difiglio, "Energy Efficiency and Consumption—the Rebound Effect—A Survey." *Energy Policy* 28: 389-401.

[11] Turner

IV. Intermediaries in the Workforce Development System

DEMETRA SMITH NIGHTINGALE, PH.D.

In the workforce development world, there is a growing recognition of the importance of intermediaries in the implementation of programs. National organizations such as the National Urban League, with affiliates that are local workforce development intermediaries, are an important part of the nation's workforce development system and are uniquely positioned to ensure the effective provision of employment and training services at the community level.

As Congress considers reauthorizing both the Workforce Investment Act (WIA) and the Temporary Assistance for Needy Families (TANF) program in 2010, it is useful to define and examine the role of intermediaries, what they are, and their current and future responsibilities.

Intermediaries Defined

While the term is used by many policy makers, program administrators and staff, and even by journalists in the popular press, there is no single definition of an "intermediary" in workforce development. In a general sense, an intermediary is an entity or individual that acts as a mediator or serves at an intermediate stage between two or more parties or two or more actions. Intermediaries are found in many public program contexts.

TWO TYPES OF WORKFORCE DEVELOPMENT INTERMEDIARIES

Labor Exchange Services Intermediary: a program, company, organization, or person that acts as a link between a job seeker and employer.

Examples: Public Job Service Office or One Stop Career Center, Union Hiring Hall, Private Personnel Agency, Non-Profit Employment and Training Organization, Job Counselor, Job Placement Specialist, Account Executive

Institutional or Administrative Intermediary: a program, company, agency, or organization that acts on behalf of a government agency, usually under contract, to provide labor exchange services or other employment-related services to clients seeking employment.

Examples: WIA Service Provider, TANF Work Program Service Provider, One-Stop Career Center Operator

---

Perhaps the most common and formal use of the term in public policy circles occurs in health care. In Medicare and Medicaid, organizations or companies have contractual arrangements with the government or with private businesses to serve as fiscal intermediaries, processing and managing health enrollments, claims, and payments. In child welfare, senior services, mental health, and even criminal justice contexts, individuals may serve as advocates or intermediaries to help with daily activities or arrange services for those unable to effectively arrange services for themselves.

Intermediaries also exist in the context of the private labor market, primarily linking job seekers with potential employers. Private personnel agencies, for example, are often contractually engaged by businesses to recruit and screen for new employees, or to provide temporary employees. Those agencies may also market their services to both job seekers and businesses that are hiring permanent or temporary workers, with one or both parties paying the fee for those services. Labor unions also serve as employment intermediaries, operating union hiring halls and registries where members can connect to job openings, and sponsoring apprenticeships.

This labor intermediation function between workers and employers also occurs in public programs. Free labor exchange services, for example, are available to all job seekers and employers through the public system of employment services authorized under the Wagner-Peyser Act of 1933. Over the years, these services have been provided locally through offices variously referred to as the Employment Service or the Job Service and now typically integrated into the national network of One Stop Career Centers defined in the Workforce Investment Act. Since 1933, public employees funded under the federal Wagner-Peyser legislation have served as labor market intermediaries—go-betweens—linking job seekers and employers in the labor exchange process. In both private personnel agency and public employment service transactions, it is common for the employment or placement professional to stay in contact with the employer and the person placed to assure the match has been appropriate, mediate any issues that arise, and sometimes replace a person if it turns out the match is not appropriate.

Local Workforce Development Intermediaries
Any program that provides employment-related services incorporates labor exchange services, matching job seekers and employers. Many programs target particular population groups, and most programs provide support services, job training, or education in addition to job placement. For example, programs that target specific populations of job seekers such as welfare recipients, youth, older workers, veterans, women reentering the labor market, persons with disabilities, immigrants, dislocated workers, individuals being released from jail or prison, and many other groups often involve some type of employment-related services. Programs or agencies responsible for such programs either deliver the employment services themselves (in-house) or, more often, contract with other agencies or service providers to deliver the employment services.[1] Whether provided in-house or contracted out, those programs (and the staff in them) function as labor market intermediaries, performing tasks that link or match individuals seeking work with businesses that are seeking employees.

However, in programs serving individuals who may have special or unique employment-related issues or needs, the role of these intermediary organizations is broader and more complex than just the labor exchange activity one might see in a personnel agency or hiring hall. A program may provide clients with employment services along with other services such as child care, transportation, social services, crisis intervention, help in overcoming problems related to housing, health, substance abuse, or domestic violence, or addressing educational or job skills deficiencies. Staff may provide these various services themselves ("in-house") or they may refer clients to other specialty provider organizations. In other words, they serve as intermediaries between their job-seeking clients and potential employers as well as

---

TYPES OF LOCAL WORKFORCE DEVELOPMENT PROGRAM INTERMEDIARIES

1. Independent service provider entities & companies
   » *Private company*
   » *Non-profit organization*

2. Affiliated service provider entities that are part of a network, organization, company, or association
   » *Local non-profit affiliates of a national organization such as the National Urban League*
   » *Independent non-profit organizations in a local or regional network or association*
   » *Local unions*
   » *Local operations of a for-profit company*
   » *Local public programs and offices of a government agency*

---

intermediaries between their clients and needed services provided by other agencies.

There is also an institutional dimension to intermediaries. In addition to serving as labor market intermediaries between individuals and employers, the staff in employment-providing programs may also operate as administrative intermediaries, linking their own program or organizations with other programs and organizations, sometimes with financial agreements. For example, to serve as effective brokers of services for their clients, programs must have procedures in place for referring clients, purchasing or otherwise arranging for services, tracking services, and the like. Public agencies may also have contractual or non-contractual arrangements with public, non-profit, or private entities to provide particular services. Those outside (usually contracted) entities serve as intermediaries between the public agency or government and the individual clients for whom the agency is responsible.

Thus, the term "intermediary" in workforce development programming can include activities that range from general labor exchange and job matching to much more complex roles that include service brokering for clients (job seekers) with the ultimate goal of facilitating a successful job match, and institutional arrangements where one entity is contracted to provide particular services for another entity. Several types of intermediaries exist because of this wide range of activities involved in workforce development. It helps to think about two general categories of intermediaries in the workforce development system: independent entities that provide direct employment-related services, and entities that are affiliated with a network or national organization, such as the National Urban League, Opportunities Industrialization Centers (OIC), Goodwill Industries, and SER-Jobs for Progress, and the International Association of Jewish Vocational Services (among others).

Non-profit community based intermediaries have been important service delivery agents in employment and training programs for many decades. In addition to receiving contracts from state or local agencies to serve as labor market intermediaries for various programs, community-based employment organizations have often received direct funding from the federal government. In the 1960s and 1970s, for example, many community-based organizations received federal employment and training funds directly from the U.S. Department of Labor. Non-profit intermediaries were particularly common for youth employment and job training services including summer youth employment programs, school-to-work programs, job training, work experience, remedial education, mentoring and after-school programs.[2]

Nonprofit community-based organizations, in general, also are viewed as filling needs or providing services not fully developed by public agencies or private for-profit businesses.[3] Non-profit employment providers are considered especially important for reaching and serving some of the most disadvantaged workers that might otherwise have limited access to publicly-funded programs, including youth, low-skilled workers, older workers, and some ethnic and cultural groups. During the period following the major federal welfare reforms in the late 1990s, community-based organizations were called upon to play a major role in moving individuals from welfare to work and hundreds of organizations received direct funding from the U.S. Department of Labor to operate programs for welfare recipients, non-custodial parents and others at risk of going onto the welfare rolls. More recently the Labor Department's Pathways out of Poverty Grants include direct grants to many community-based organizations in addition to community colleges, local government, workforce investment boards, and other providers of training.

Role of National Intermediary Organizations

Many independent community organizations that function as labor market intermediaries operate locally on their own, developing partnerships with agencies and employers, bidding for service delivery contracts and seeking other operating funds for their organizations from various sources including federal and state government agencies and private philanthropic foundations.

SOME IMPORTANT ROLES OF NATIONAL WORKFORCE DEVELOPMENT INTERMEDIARIES

» **Targeting**: Improved targeting to low income communities and job seekers and expanded employment and training opportunities, particularly for minority groups

» **Capacity Building**: Building and maintaining program service delivery capacity of local labor market intermediaries, particularly those serving low income communities that might otherwise lack effective services

» **Rapid Implementation**: Facilitating the rapid implementation of federal initiatives, especially new policies and crisis response activities

In addition, hundreds of local non-profit employment intermediaries are affiliated with national organizations such as the National Urban League and others mentioned above. These national intermediary organizations represent another partner in the workforce development system, and they serve complementary purposes that can strengthen the capacity of local service delivery and labor exchange intermediaries.

The role and unique contribution that national intermediary organizations make in the workforce development system are important to note, particularly in terms of targeting low-income communities and persons, building and maintaining local service delivery capacity, and facilitating rapid implementation of federal initiatives.

Funding through national organizations can improve targeting and expand services to low-income communities and job seekers locally.
When national organizations receive funding from a federal agency or from philanthropic foundations for service delivery, their involvement can complement and enhance federal funding that is allocated through state and local agencies. For example, the Senior Community Service Employment Program for older workers, administered by the Labor Department, has 18 national grantees, including the National Urban League, selected competitively in addition to funding to state agencies responsible for aging programs. The Labor Department's new Federal Pathways Out of Poverty grants have also been awarded to several national intermediary organizations including OIC and SER, to coordinate programming by some of their local intermediary affiliates. The proposed American Graduation Initiative is also likely to include some emphasis on expanding job training and education opportunities to low income youth and adults, increasing the total amount of federal funding available for such activities and the proportion of funds devoted to education and training for those groups.[4] Federal grants to national intermediary organizations can be an efficient way to distribute some federal funds to effective local intermediate affiliates to ensure that minorities and low-income persons have access to the expanded programs,

and provides a mechanism of accountability back to the federal agency. That is, funding national intermediary organizations can support both types of intermediary models: labor market intermediaries at the local level, and administrative/fiscal intermediaries at the national level.

National intermediary organizations provide a mechanism for building and maintaining the capacity of local affiliate service providers. National organizations, for example, arrange opportunities to share information about best practices, sponsoring forums for information clearinghouses through on-line technologies and at national and regional conferences. Technical assistance projects also provide an important way for local affiliates to receive state-of-the guidance and training to improve local intermediary activities. Local community-based organizations can be outside of the mainstream communications of local government programs because they often work intensively in poor communities. Being affiliated with a national organization and using the communication channels of that national network serve a critically important information role for the programs on the ground.

National intermediary organizations can facilitate the rapid implementation of federal initiatives. National organizations can be very important when rapid response is important because they have established networks and methods for communicating to the field. They can be intermediaries between the federal government and community action. For example, during the current deep recession and the need to move quickly to implement provisions of the Recovery Act

national organizations can collaborate with federal agencies to communicate quickly to the field, allocate funds to local areas, and otherwise infuse new federal policy directives quickly. Of course, they cannot replace the federal-state-local mechanisms, but national organizations can be an important partner in rapid implementation. Rapid response is also critical after disasters, as occurred in the Gulf coast in 2005 after Hurricanes Katrina and Rita. National organizations can help facilitate implementation of federal policies when time is of the essence.

Conclusion
National organizations with affiliate networks represent both types of intermediary models in the workforce development system. They function as networks for grassroots labor market intermediaries, particularly for the low income and minority community, and they also function as administrative and fiscal intermediaries between the federal government and local communities helping improve targeting to low income workers and communities, building the capacity of workforce development service delivery in those communities, and facilitating the rapid implementation of federal policies when timely response is critical.

The unique role of national intermediary organizations in workforce development policy should be recognized as Congress considers WIA reauthorization. A two-pronged community-based grants program should be established to provide resources to: 1) local intermediaries; and 2) national organizations with local operational program affiliates.

The goals for the national workforce intermediary grants should be to facilitate technical assistance, coordinate peer-exchanges around best practice service delivery and population targeting approaches, and establish timely procedures to feed back information about implementation to the federal government. An investment of this type would capitalize on the added value that national organizations can bring to the nation's workforce development system.

NOTES

[1] LaDonna Pavetti, Michelle K. Derr, Jaquelyn Anderson, Carole Trippe, and Sidnee Paschal, "Changing the Culture of Welfare Offices: The Role of Intermediaries in Linking TANF Recipients with Jobs," Federal Reserve Bank of New York, *Economic Policy Review*, September 2001.

[2] Demetra S. Nightingale and Carolyn Taylor O'Brien, *Community Based Organizations in the Job Training Partnership System*, Urban Institute Project Report to the Ford Foundation, October 1984.

[3] Burton Weisbrod, "The Role of the Nonprofit Sector", Focus, University of Wisconsin Institute for Research on Poverty, 2002; and *The Privatization of Social Services: A Background Paper*, Nancy Pindus and Demetra Smith Nightingale, U.S. Department of Labor, Office of the Assistant Secretary for Policy, October 1997.

[4] Kelly Mikelson and Demetra Nightingale, *Estimating Public and Private Expenditures on Occupational Training in the United States*, Urban Institute report to the U.S. Department of Labor, Employment and Training Administration 2004.

V. Education: The Path to Success for African Americans

EDUCATION SECRETARY ARNE DUNCAN

As our country is emerging from the worst recession in a generation, there's one lesson we have learned: Education matters more than ever. Throughout the recession, those who have a bachelor's degree faired much better than high school dropouts. Now we know for certain that education is the one true path out of poverty and into economic security. It's the reason that education is the civil rights issue of our time.

As a country, we profess that children shouldn't be denied a world-class education based on the color of their skin, their family's income, or their zip code. But the promise of a world-class education system is being deferred for African Americans all across the country.

The evidence is shocking. The achievement gap is unacceptably large. The average black child is two or three grade levels behind the average white child. About half our African American students fail to graduate on time. Only one in five blacks over the age of 25 has a bachelor's degree. Without a college degree, African Americans aren't prepared a future where they will prosper, become leaders of their communities, and be leaders for the next generation. In short, too many in the black community are being denied the American dream. Solving the problem starts with improving education.

We are starting to see excellent results in some schools serving African Americans in some of the toughest neighborhoods. They are enrolling students who are mostly black and mostly poor. Most of these students are reading below grade level when they enter. After a few years, those same students are passing state tests at rates unheard of in neighborhood schools. In these schools, the leaders are telling their students that they will graduate and go to college. Most of them fulfill that dream. Right now, these schools are the exception. But we know that schools such as Urban Prep in Chicago, the Harlem Children Zone Promise Academy in New York City, and the Achievable Dream Academy in Newport News, Virginia, are preparing their students for success in life. The biggest question facing education today

is: Now that we know what success looks like, why do we tolerate failure? And the biggest question facing the black community is: How can we help these schools and their students thrive and envision a future where they are full participants in America's economic and political life?

The educational success of African-American students isn't simply a concern for the black community. It's an issue that all Americans must address. Last year, McKenzie & Company estimated that our gross domestic product would have been up to $525 billion higher each year if we closed the achievement gap. The gap is large enough to cause what McKenzie characterized as "a permanent national recession." Other researchers say the lack of educational opportunity takes a toll on the greater economy. High school dropouts are more likely to go to jail, have higher health care costs, and require greater government assistance than high school graduates. Solving the education crisis in the black community is a concern for every American.

President Obama has a cradle-to-career agenda that will reform our schools and improve the educational outcomes for all of our students, particularly those who are poor and disadvantaged.

The agenda starts with $9.3 billion over the next decade for early learning programs. We'll create incentives for states to improve the quality of their programs so their students are prepared to succeed in kindergarten.

In K-12 education, we're supporting reforms through the Race to the Top program and the reauthorization of the No Child Left Behind Act.

We want states to raise their standards so all students will be prepared to succeed in college and careers. For too long, states have lowered their expectations and their students haven't been prepared to succeed once their graduate. That has to change. To do that, we know that we'll need our best teachers where they're needed the most—in classrooms where students are struggling. We will reward educators who are doing the best jobs of improving student achievement—especially those working in high-poverty schools. And we're making an unprecedented investment in efforts to turn around our lowest-performing schools. We have more than $3.5 billion available to find new leaders for these schools to transform them from dropout factories to models of success.

The final piece of the agenda will make college affordable for all. We'll end taxpayers' subsidies for banks and invest in our students by increasing aid and lowering student loan payments. Under our plan, we will guarantee that Pell Grants—the largest federal student aid program—will increase at the rate of inflation plus one percent every year. Student loan borrowers will pay no more than 10 percent of their monthly income. Their debt will be forgiven after 20 years—10 years if they are a teacher, police officer, or some other public servant. It's the biggest investment in higher education since the GI Bill. Everyone who wants to go to college should be able to afford college. This bill takes big steps to make that happen.

President Obama and I are dedicated to reforming education because it is a moral obligation and an economic imperative. We're providing unprecedented resources and we are expecting transformational change—the types of changes that will accelerate the achievement of black children so they graduate from high school and are ready to succeed in college and the workforce.

> ...create a world in which our black children can see models of success in executive suites, in politics, and local businesses.

For our agenda to succeed, we will need the help of community leaders who rally around our students and support their success. I'm challenging all members of the black community to make a difference in the lives of children, day in and day out, and I'm challenging political leaders at every level to create a world in which our black children can see models of success in executive suites, in politics, and local businesses.

At the Urban Prep High Schools in Chicago, every school year begins with a convocation ceremony. The highlight of the ceremony is when black men stand before the school of black boys and pledge to support them. In the oath, these successful black men say: "We believe that you will finish college and that you know you can do so because we stand before you as living proof of what can be done." They also promise to work closely with students throughout the year, tutoring them, mentoring them, and making sure they are doing the hard work so they graduate and go to college.

We need more schools and community members working together to support our students in this way. But those support networks need to go beyond schools. They must extend to pastors, coaches, bus drivers—anyone in the community or in schools who can make a difference in the lives of students. The whole community needs to be an extended family, sending students a message that their path to success starts with education. These leaders also need to ensure our children are living in safe neighborhoods. Today, too many of our black children live in communities plagued by violence. Children from those neighborhoods have told me the career they want to pursue "if they grow up," not "when they grow up." How can we expect them to study hard and dream big if they don't think they'll live past the age of 18?

These are leadership opportunities for the black community. But we need the corporate community to lead as well. For too many black youth, the only successful role models are athletes and entertainers. As someone who played basketball all of my life, I know how hard it is to make it in the NBA. For all of the hard work I put into my game, the closest I got was a tryout for the Boston Celtics. Many of the guys I played against growing up in Chicago never got that close. They played ball for their high schools and college, but never got the education they needed to succeed. They learned the hard way that the NBA—or any other professional sport—is out of reach for the vast majority of our youth. They need other visions of success.

Today, they don't see role models in corporate boardrooms, law firms, and other professional fields. Because many businesses and jobs have moved out of urban America, these youth don't even have examples of insurance salesmen, bank tellers, and small business owners. These jobs may not provide the prestige and wealth of professional sports or corporate leadership. But they are a ticket to the middle class and financial security. We need black leaders in these types of jobs—from the corporate boardroom to the community business owner. If our black youth do not see models of success, they don't have any reason to work hard, do their homework, and finish school. They'll continue to dream of a life that's not attainable, instead of dedicating themselves to the getting the education they need to succeed in the American economy.

President Obama and I believe that the future of our black youth is a concern not just for African Americans. It's a concern for all Americans. It's our responsibility as leaders to make sure every child in this country has the best education the world has to offer. It's a responsibility for professional educators and all members of the black community. It's going to take all of us working together, challenging each other, and doing what's best for the black boys and girls who have the potential to be our leaders tomorrow. We should begin by improving our schools and supporting our young children in their education.

VI. Jobs & Healthcare:
An Alternative
"Public Option"

DARRICK HAMILTON, PH.D., ARTHUR H. GOLDSMITH, PH.D.,
AND WILLIAM DARITY, JR., PH.D.

Over 45 million Americans face the prospect of becoming sick and confronting expensive medical costs without the financial security of health insurance coverage. This is particularly true for black Americans, whose 2006 (before the current financial crisis) median net worth of about $12,000—which is less than ten percent of the comparable white values of $121,000—offers them very little financial security to deal with sicknesses. Indeed, 28 percent of black households, compared to 16 percent for white households, have zero or negative net worth.[1]

Studies show that blacks and Latinos are less likely than non-Latino-whites to have health insurance coverage, even after accounting for a wide range of factors.[2] The 2007 U.S. Census Bureau's Current Population Survey reveals that the annual uninsurance rates for blacks is about 21 percent—almost double the 12 percent rate for whites—while Latinos have the highest uninsurance rate at 34 percent. Some of these insurance discrepancies can be explained by the socioeconomic positioning of these groups. For example, blacks and Latinos are disproportionately employed in service occupations that exhibit low rates of insurance coverage relative to managerial and professional work where they are underrepresented. However, even within occupational categories, the uninsurance rates for blacks and Latinos exceed those of their white peers, suggesting that actions across firms may be a source of their low insurance coverage rates.

This essay offers evidence that the racial composition of a firm's workforce influences whether it offers employees health insurance coverage. We find that employment at firms with predominantly white workforces are associated with a higher likelihood of employer-sponsored health insurance, and firms with predominantly non-white workforces are associated with a lower likelihood, both relative to racially diverse firms, even after controlling for a large set of known determinants of employer-sponsored health insurance. In addition, firms with predominantly male workforces have a greater proclivity to offer insurance than those that are largely female.

Despite this, there may still be some room for optimism. The federal government is now engaged in serious debate to reform the health insurance system. Several options are being considered including: mandated coverage with non-compliance penalties for both employers and individuals, insurance exchanges for small businesses and individuals to come together and benefit from risk pooling, the use of the tax code to provide health insurance subsidies to small businesses and both low and middle income individuals, Medicaid expansions, insurance regulations that cap beneficiary out-of-pocket expenses, define minimum coverages and prohibit the denial of coverage for pre-existing medical conditions, and public insurance options that provide alternatives for consumers and, through market competition discipline private insurers to provide quality health insurance plans. However, despite this myriad of reform options, the foundation of a U.S. employer-sponsored health insurance system is not expected to change.

We therefore propose a more comprehensive approach to addressing this problem: an "alternative public option" that will dramatically reduce the number of uninsured Americans and the accompanying racial health disparities and lead to a full employment U.S. economy.

We use data drawn from the Multi-City Telephone Employer Survey (MCTES), to explore the influence of racial workforce composition on firm provision of health insurance. The MCTES is a cross-sectional telephone based survey collected between 1992 and 1995 and administered in the metropolitan areas of Atlanta, Boston, Detroit and Los Angeles. The data focuses on hiring and vacancies at firms that primarily employ non-college degree workers.[4] Our primary

Table 1: *Percent of Firm Offering Health Insurance Coverage by Racial, Ethnic, and Gender Composition of the Non-College Educated Workers at a Firm*

WHITE WORKFORCE COMPOSITION	SHARE OF FIRMS		SHARE OF FIRMS OFFERING COVERAGE	
	Male	Female	Male	Female
None	0.15	0.12	0.58	0.56
1-9 Percent	0.11	0.12	0.81	0.83
10-49 Percent	0.37	0.38	0.80	0.82
At Least 50 Percent	0.24	0.24	0.77	0.72
Missing	0.13	0.13	0.86	0.86

variable of interest is whether a firm offers health insurance to its last employee hired for a position that does not require a college degree.

We identify the racial composition of the firm's workforce separately for males and for females by specifying the following five categories of firm composition: (a) no whites, (b) 1-9 percent white, (c) 10-49 percent white, (d) at least half white, and (e) a category control for missing, unresponsive or undefined firm respondents.[5] Thus, the first category is indicative of a completely non-white segregated workforce, the third category, 10-49 percent white, indicates a racially mixed category, and the fourth category represents a predominantly white workforce.[6]

The first two columns of *Table 1* display the racial composition of firm male and female workforces in our sample, while the last two columns indicate the health insurance offer rates for firms at various levels of racial compositions. For both the male and female workforce distributions, 24 percent of the firms in our sample had at least a 50 percent white workforce, while 15 and 12 percents had, respectively, no white employees. In terms of health insurance offer rates, respectively, 77 and 72 percent of majority white male and female workforce firms offered their last employee health insurance, while only 58 and 56 percent of firms with no white males and females (i.e. exclusively non-white firms) did. This is a respective 22 and 16 percentage point difference in offer rates between firms with workforces that are largely white and completely non-white.

There are a number of explanations for why comparable non-white firms might offer less coverage than white firms. Among the possible explanations are (1) higher premiums faced by firms to cover workers from non-white groups due to lower health status, (2) lower profitability of these non-white firms, (3) lower collective bargaining power to negotiate health insurance coverage for workers at firms that employ relatively more black and Latino employees, (4) lower demand for coverage from predominantly black and Latino workforces, and, lastly, (5) workers employed at firms with large shares of non-white workers may be more susceptible to structural barriers unrelated to their work characteristics such as labor market discrimination and as a result be offered less insurance coverage.[7]

Table 2: *Probit Estimates of Probability of Firm Offering Employees Health Insurance by Firm: Workforce Racial Composition (Summary Table)**

VARIABLES	POOLED DATA	
	Model A (n=3053)	Model B (n=2989)
Male Workforce Racial Composition		
No White Males	-.025 (.025)	-.026 (.025)
1-9% White Male	-.022 (.028)	-.019 (.027)
At Least 50% White Male	.038* (.019)	.042** (.019)
Missing White Male Composition	.134 (.061)	.120 (.071)
Female Workforce Racial Composition		
No White Females	-.028 (.027)	-.029 (.027)
1-9% White Female	-.022 (.028)	-.017 (.028)
At Least 50% White Female	-.017 (.022)	-.024 (.022)
Missing White Female Composition	-.094 (.133)	-.049 (.132)
F-Tests for Combined Male and Female Subcategories		
No White Male and No White Female	2.82* [0.093]	3.01* [0.083]
1-9 % White Male and 1-9% White Female	1.65 [0.200]	1.08 [0.299]
At Least 50% White Male and at Least 50% White Female	0.50 [0.479]	0.38 [0.537]
F-Tests for Gender Difference		
No White Male vs. No White Female	0.01 [0.931]	0.01 [0.942]
1-9 % White Male vs. 1-9% White Female	0.00 [0.998]	0.00 [0.971]
At Least 50% White Male vs at Least 50% White Female	4.28** [0.039]	5.97** [0.015]
Chi Square Stat	720***	719***
Pseudo R2	.22	.23

*Notes: Columns report marginal probit estimates evaluated at mean values for all the included variables (see *Appendix Table 2* for estimates of all included variable) of the likelihood of firms offering insurance to the last employee hired, standard errors are reported in parentheses. Specification A is our preferred model, while Specification B contains some variables that might be endogenous such as firm performance in the past year and over a longer span of time. The "White Model" controls for composition of white employees at the firm while the "Nonwhite Model" controls for composition of black and Latino employees at the firm.

Moreover, there are many other factors that are expected to affect whether a firm makes health insurance coverage available to its workers, some of which may be related to the racial composition of the workforce. Therefore, we estimate a probit likelihood function in order to isolate the marginal effect of the racial composition of a firm's workforce on its provision of health insurance from other potential explanatory factors.

Table 2 presents these marginal contributions of firm racial composition after controlling for an array of factors (see *Appendix Table 1* for variable definitions of the control variables and *Appendix Table 2* for the full results of our probit models). A connection between firm size and the likelihood of providing health insurance to workers can be identified from a number of different channels. For instance, larger firms may be able to purchase insurance at a lower price. Also, workers may prefer employment in smaller establishments. Thus, larger firms may feel compelled to offer health insurance as a fringe benefit to compensate for their greater size when searching for employees. Also, large firms allow for risk pooling, which can lower the average cost of insurance. Thus, the control variables include a string of indicators to categorize a firm's size.

Firms may be less inclined to offer health insurance to workers who are not permanent full-time employees, since these workers may leave the firm prematurely. Moreover, firms may attempt to avoid the cost of providing health insurance by hiring part-time, seasonal or contractual workers, who typically receive less fringe compensation. Thus, in our empirical work we control for these alternative types of work arrangements.

We also control for a percent of the firm's workforce that is covered by a collective bargaining agreement (unionized), which is highly correlated with firm provisions for health insurance. In addition, there are controls for the non-college degree and non-high school degree portions of a firm's workforce. Workforce occupation is controlled based on proportion of clerical, sales and blue collar workers at a firm. We also include indicators of the firm's industry based on first digit census SIC codes; an indicator for if the firm is for-profit; and an indicator for if the firm has multiple worksites or not. Finally, we include geographical controls for metropolitan area (Atlanta, Boston, Detroit or Los Angeles) of the firm, whether the firm is located in a central city, and temporal controls for the year when the survey was conducted.[8]

The variables listed above coupled with the racial composition of a firm describe that firm's provisions of health insurance to its workers. This constitutes our main model, Model A, of health insurance provision. However, we also examine another model, Model B, which ignores potential estimation problems of simultaneity, by including additional indicators, like the average number of months of current vacancies at a firm and the short and long-term economic performance of the firm, which are likely to be circularly related to health insurance provision. These additional controls may insert bias into our estimates, but on the other hand, they further isolate the un-confounded effect of the racial composition of a firm on health insurance provisions. The average months of vacancies accounts for the possibility that firms offer

health insurance as a means to attract workers. The economic performance variables, whether a firm experienced a positive or negative change in the volume of its sales in the last year, and whether a firm experienced an increase or decrease in sales over the past 5-10 years, serve as profitability indicators, which in-turn may be related to a firm's willingness and ability to offer health insurance.

The control variables above allow us to better isolate the effects of workforce racial composition on firm health insurance provisions from three out of the five possible explanations listed above. The first explanation is that white firms may face lower insurance premiums leading to greater provision of health insurance as result of risk-pooling, economies of scale, and a better workforce health status. These firm attributes are likely to be correlated with firm size and the education composition of a firm's workforce, which are controls included in our model. The second explanation is that white firms may offer more coverage because they are more profitable. In Model B, we add indicators of short and long-term sales growth, so to the extent that these measures are associated with profitability, profitability is controlled as well. The third explanation is the possibility that white firms may be more likely to be governed by a collective bargaining agreement (i.e. unionized), so we include a measure of portion of workforce governed by collective bargaining agreement as well. The remaining two explanations for why white firms may have a higher proclivity to provide health insurance are their workforce has a higher demand for coverage and/or workers in non-white firms may face higher discriminatory barriers to attaining health insurance offers. Hence, to the extent that our control variables are associated with the first three explanations, any remaining effects measured by our racial workforce indicators should serve as indicators of one of the remaining two explanations.

Table 2 presents the marginal contribution to the offer of health insurance by firms, with various proportions of white male and white female employees relative to firms that are, respectively, 10-49 percent white male and 10-49 percent white female for Model A and Model B. Thus, racially diverse firms serve as the reference group in the analysis. In addition, the last rows of the table present F-test results that allow us to examine if the marginal contribution of combined sub-categories of firm racial compositions affect firm coverage. Also, the use of F-tests permits us to determine if there are any gender differences in the impact of racial workforce composition on health insurance coverage.

Based on Model A, we find that firms with at least a 50 percent white male workforce are about 3.8 percent more likely to offer health insurance relative to racially mixed firms. Although, not statistically significant, the other coefficients based on white male workforce composition suggest that firms with no whites and less than 10 percent white workers are 2.5 and 2.2 percent less likely to offer coverage. None of the female workforce compositions are statistically significant, but in all cases racially diverse female firms are more likely to offer coverage. Further, the F-tests in the bottom panel reveal that firms with a combination of no white males or females are significantly less likely to offer health insurance. Both of these

results are consistent with our hypothesis that white as opposed to non-white workforces are more likely to be offered health insurance even after controlling for a long list of variables.

Finally, the F-tests in the table also examine gender differences. We find that majority white male firms are significantly more likely to offer insurance than majority white female worker firms. Hence, both the gender and racial composition of a firms non-college educated workforce are estimated to influence health insurance provision. Moreover, when measures of average months of vacancies, and short-run and long-run sales growth are added as controls (Model B), there are no substantive differences to any of the results described above.

The new agency would guarantee a job for every American seeking work.

In the midst of this Great Recession, the January 2010 unemployment rates for whites stood at 8.7 percent, and at 16.5 percent—nearly twice as high—for blacks (based on the U.S. Census' Current Populations Survey). In addition, there are large racial disparities in workers who have dropped out of the workforce altogether due to discouragement from prolonged bouts of unemployment.[9] Finally, the systemic structures that lead to racial sorting with respect occupations also highlights the limitation of reform that maintains an employer-sponsored system as its core. Hamilton (2006) finds that over 85 percent of U.S. occupations are characterized by racial over-representation (typically blacks in low earning occupations and whites in high earning occupations), even after accounting for occupational educational attainment requirements. Moreover, at the 2010 annual Allied Social Science Association/ National Economics Association meetings, we presented a paper that indicates that health insurance coverage is also related to racial occupation concentrations with blacks typically crowded into lower coverage occupations.

However, given this link between the racial composition of firms and their provisions for health insurance, we need to acknowledge the limitations of the health insurance reform options that are currently being considered. The options all center around a system that maintains employer-sponsored health insurance as its cornerstone. These limitations are further heightened when we consider other employment related sources of insurance disparities such as differentials in rates of employment.

Hence, it seems unlikely that health insurance reforms that the president and Congress are currently considering will lead to coverage for all Americans, particularly, given the ongoing racial stratifications in employment.

There is, however, an "alternative public option" that would more dramatically reduce the number of uninsured Americans and the accompanying racial disparity in coverage resulting from these stratifications: a National Investment Employment Agency modeled similar to the Civilian Conservation Corps (CCC) enacted in 1936 during the Great Depression. This alternative would not only result in more Americans being insured

and reduce racial disparities in coverage, it would help rebuild America's crumbling infrastructure, while putting millions of Americans, regardless of race, to work. The new agency would guarantee a job for every American seeking work.[10] The federal government would serve as an employer of last resort in both good and bad economic times.

Not only would this "alternative public option" include a health insurance benefits plan that extends the health care security that is available to U.S. Members of Congress and other federal civil servants, it would fulfill the promise and the intent of the Humphrey Hawkins Act: a federal job guarantee that leads to the establishment of a permanent full employment U.S. economy.

BIBLIOGRAPHY

Achiron, Marilyn "Fighting Poverty at Work" *OECD Observer* No. 274 October 2009 pp.13-14.

Bergmann, Barbara R. 1971. "The Effect on White Incomes of Discrimination in Employment" *Journal of Political Economy* 29(2): 294-313.

Becker, Becker, Garry S. 1957. *The Economics of Discrimination.* Chicago: University of Chicago Press.

Crow, S. E., M. E. Harrington, and C. G. McLaughlin. 2002. *Health Insurance and Vulnerable Populations: Racial and Ethnic Minorities, Immigrants, and People with Chronic Mental Illness.* Background Paper, Economic Research Initiative on the Uninsured, University of Michigan (October 14, 2002).

Goldsmith, Arthur; Jonathan Veum, and William Darity Jr."Unemployment, Joblessness, Psychological Well-Being and Full Employment: Theory and Evidence" *Journal of Socio-economics* 26:2 1997 pp.133-158.

Hall, A., Scott Collins, and S. Glied, 1999. *Employer Sponsored Health Insurance: Implications for Minority Workers.* The Commonwealth Fund.

Hamilton, Darrick. 2006. "The Racial Composition of American Jobs" edited by George Curry: *The 2006 State of Black America.* The National Urban League.

Harvey, Philip *Securing the Right to Full Employment: Social Welfare Policy and the Unemployed in the United States* Princeton: Princeton University Press 1989.

Harvey, Philip "Direct Job Creation" in Aaron Warner (ed.) *The Commitment to Full Employment* Armonk: M.E. Sharpe 2000 pp.35-54.

Holzer, Harry. 1996. *What Employers Want: Job Prospects for Less-Educated Workers.* New York: Russell Sage Foundation.

Institute of Medicine. 2001. *Coverage Matters: Insurance and Health Care.* Committee on the Consequences of Uninsurance, Board on Health Care Services.

Ku, L., and S. Matani. 2001. Let out: Immigrants' Access to Health Care and Insurance. *Health Affairs* 20(1), 247-56.

Morrissey, M.B. "Open Letter to President Barack Obama", February 7, 2010. Shi, L., 2000. Vulnerable Populations and Health Insurance. *Medical Care Research and Review*, 57(1), 110-34.

Wray, L. Randall "Job Guarantee" in William Darity Jr. (ed.) *International Encyclopedia of the Social Sciences* Vol.4 Detroit: Thomson Gale (Macmillan Reference USA) 2008 pp.204-206.

Wray, L. Randall and Mathew Forstater "Full Employment and Social Justice" in Dell Champlin and Janet Knoedler (eds.) *The Institutionalist Tradition in Labor Economics* Armonk: M.E. Sharpe 2004 pp.253-272.

NOTES

We would like to thank Economic Research Initiative on the Uninsured, University of Michigan and the Robert Wood Johnson Foundation for providing generous support. In addition, this research has benefited from helpful comments from conference participants at the Economic Research Initiative on the Uninsured's Conference on Vulnerable Populations (October, 2004), the Association of Public Policy and Management's Annual Meetings (November, 2004), and the Southern Economic Association's Annual Meetings (November, 2004). Any mistakes are the sole responsibility of the authors.

[1] The net worth figures are based on the U.S. Census Bureau's Survey of Income and Program Participation.

[2] See Crow, Harrington, and McLaughlin (2002) for a survey of what is known about the link between race, ethnicity, immigrant status and insurance coverage.

[3] Observations from larger firms had a higher likelihood of being included in the sample. This sampling technique accounts for the otherwise under-representation of workers at large firms. The over-sampling of large firms creates a better depiction of the typical (average) worker since larger firms contain more workers. Also, the surveys emphasis on non-college degree workers permits a focus on workers that are more likely to be uninsured.

The analysis is based on 3,053 firms. Firm information is provided by either the owner, Director of Human Resources, or another high level manager. The data set began with information on 3,510 firms, but 467 firms were not included because we did not have information on all the variables used in our formal analysis. Fourteen firms were lost due to lack of information on health insurance provisions, 259 for missing responses on the number of employees at the firm, and 184 for lack of information on percent of workforce that is unionized.

[4] Although gender is not of primary interest in this paper we have chosen not to combine males and females in order to allow for the possibility that racial firm composition exhibits differential effects on insurance offerings based on gender. We rely on F-test to examine the combined effects of white male and female firm composition as well as the differential effects associated with gender.

[5] The use of categories rather than a continuous variable of racial and ethnic composition allows for easier analytical interpretation, gets at threshold and non-linear effects and, by including a category for missing observations, avoid the loss of observations from which we had missing information.

[6] There are several ways in which discrimination may manifest. For example, bigoted employers may appease there "taste" for discrimination by offering employees at firms with large non-white workforces low rates of coverage (see Becker 1956 for an analysis of wage discrimination based on employer "taste" for discrimination). Alternatively, Barbara Bergmann (1971) presents an "occupational crowding" model of discrimination in which the wages of black workers are suppressed by crowding them into less desirable jobs. Her model can be extended to describe how non-white workers can be crowded into jobs that do not offer health insurance. We do not present a formal model of discrimination in firm health insurance offers, however, we do empirically investigate if this is a mechanism for racial inequities in coverage rates.

[7] The central city indicator is constructed based on firm mailing address, and it may not necessarily be based on its physical location.

[8] In addition, Goldsmith, Veum, and Darity (1997) discuss the psychological (mental health) effects associated with this discouraged worker phenomenon.

[9] See, Darity, *forthcoming* in the *Review of Black Political Economy* for details concerning this proposal.

*Appendix Table 1: Definition of Variables Used in the Econometric Analysis**

VARIABLES	VARIABLE DEFINITIONS	VARIABLES	VARIABLE DEFINITIONS
Insurance	1 if firm offered health insurance to the last hired non-college degree worker, 0 otherwise	Employ >250	1 if total number of permanent full-time employees at the firm is >250, 0 otherwise
Insurance Fam	1 if firm offered health insurance to a family member of the last hired non-college degree worker, 0 otherwise	Part Employ	Total number of part-time permanent employees at the firm
No White Males	1 if white male workers comprise 0% of the firms non-college degree workforce, 0 otherwise	Season Employ	Total number of seasonal, but permanent, employees at the firm
		Temp Employ	Total number of temporary full-time employees at the firm
1-9% White Male	1 if white male workers comprise 1-9% of the firms non-college degree workforce, 0 otherwise	Contract Employ	Total number of contract full-time employees at the firm
10-49% White Male	1 if white male workers comprise 10-49% of the firms non-college degree workforce, 0 otherwise	Union	% of the firms non-college degree workforce that is unionized
At least 50% White Male	1 if white male workers comprise at least 50% of the firms non-college degree workforce, 0 otherwise	For Profit	1 if firm is for profit, 0 otherwise
		Mult Worksites	1 if the firm has more than 1 worksite, 0 otherwise
Missing White Male Composition	1 if firm does not report white male workers % of the firms non-college degree workforce, 0 otherwise	Central City	1 if the firm is located in the central city, 0 otherwise
No White Females	1 if white male workers comprise 0% of the firms non-college degree workforce, 0 otherwise	Atlanta	1 if the firm is located in Atlanta, 0 otherwise
		Boston	1 if the firm is located in Boston, 0 otherwise
		Detroit	1 if the firm is located in Detroit, 0 otherwise
1-9% White Female	1 if white male workers comprise 1-9% of the firms non-college degree workforce, 0 otherwise	Los Angeles	1 if the firm is located in Los Angeles, 0 otherwise
10-49% White Female	1 if white male workers comprise 10-49% of the firms non-college degree workforce, 0 otherwise	Dropout 0	1 if 0% of the firm's non college degree workforce is composed of high school dropouts, 0 otherwise
At least 50% White Female	1 if white male workers comprise at least 50% of the firms non-college degree workforce, 0 otherwise	Dropout 1-9	1 if 1-9% of the firm's non college degree workforce is composed of high school dropouts, 0 otherwise
Missing White Female Composition	1 if firm does not report white female workers % of the firms non-college degree workforce, 0 otherwise	Dropout 10-49	1 if 10-49% of the firm's non college degree workforce is composed of high school dropouts, 0 otherwise
Employ <5	1 if total number of permanent full-time employees at the firm is <5, 0 otherwise	Dropout >49	1 if at least 50% of the firm's non college degree workforce is composed of high school dropouts, 0 otherwise
Employ 5-9	1 if total number of permanent full-time employees at the firm is between 5-9, 0 otherwise	Dropout Missing	1 if firm does not report % non college degree workforce composed of high school dropouts, 0 otherwise
Employ 10-19	1 if total number of permanent full-time employees at the firm is between 10-19, 0 otherwise	College Att 0	1 if 0% of the firm's non college degree workforce is composed of persons who at least attended college, 0 otherwise
Employ 20-49	1 if total number of permanent full-time employees at the firm is between 20-49, 0 otherwise	College Att 1-9	1 if 1-9% of the firm's non college degree workforce is at least attended college, 0 otherwise
Employ 50-99	1 if total number of permanent full-time employees at the firm is between 50-99, 0 otherwise	College Att 10-49	1 if 10-49% of the firm's non college degree workforce is composed of persons who at least attended college, 0 otherwise
Employ 100-249	1 if total number of permanent full-time employees at the firm is between 100-249, 0 otherwise	College Att >49	1 if at least 50% of the firm's non college degree workforce is composed of persons who at least attended college, 0 otherwise

Appendix Table 1: (Continued) Definition of Variables Used in the Econometric Analysis*

VARIABLES	VARIABLE DEFINITIONS
College Att Missing	1 if firm does not report % of the firm's non college degree workforce who at least attended college, 0 otherwise
Clerical 0	1 if 0% of the firm's non college degree workforce works in Clerical positions, 0 otherwise
Clerical 1-9	1 if 1-9% of the firm's non college degree workforce works in Clerical positions, 0 otherwise
Clerical 10-49	1 if 10-49 % of the firm's non college degree workforce works in Clerical positions, 0 otherwise
Clerical >49	1 if at least 50 % of the firm's non college degree workforce works in Clerical positions, 0 otherwise
Clerical Missing	1 if firm does not report % of the non college degree workforce clerical positions, 0 otherwise
Sales 0	1 if 0 % of the firm's non college degree workforce works in Sales positions, 0 otherwise
Sales 1-9	1 if 1-9% of the firm's non college degree workforce works in Sales positions, 0 otherwise
Sales 10-49	1 if 10-49 % of the firm's non college degree workforce works in Sales positions, 0 otherwise
Sales >49	1 if at least 50 % of the firm's non college degree workforce works in Sales positions, 0 otherwise
Sales Missing	1 if firm does not report % of the non college degree workforce composed of persons in sales, 0 otherwise
Blue Col 0	1 if 0 % of the firm's non college degree workforce works in Blue Collar positions, 0 otherwise
Blue Col 1-9	1 if 1-9 % of the firm's non college degree workforce works in Blue Collar positions, 0 otherwise
Blue Col 10-49	1 if 10-49 % of the firm's non college degree workforce works in Blue collar positions, 0 otherwise
Blue Col >49	1 if at least 50 % of the firm's non college degree workforce works in Blue Collar positions, 0 otherwise
Blue Col Missing	1 if firm does not report % of non college degree workforce in Blue Collar positions, 0 otherwise
Mining/Agriculture	1 if firm is in Mining or Agriculture industries, 0 otherwise
Construction	1 if firm is in Construction industry, 0 otherwise
Manufacturing	1 if firm is in Manufacturing industry, 0 otherwise

VARIABLES	VARIABLE DEFINITIONS
Transportation	1 if firm is in Transportation industry, 0 otherwise
Services	1 if firm is in Services industry, 0 otherwise
Whole Sale Trade	1 if firm is in Whole Sale Trade industry, 0 otherwise
Retail Trade	1 if firm is in Retail Trade industry, 0 otherwise
Finance	1 if firm is in Finance industry, 0 otherwise
Public Administration	1 if firm is in Public Administration industry, 0 otherwise
Industry Missing	1 if firm does not report industry in which it participates, 0 otherwise
Interview Yr 1	1 if firm representative is interviewed between June 1, 1992 and May 31 1993, 0 otherwise
Interview Yr 2	1 if firm representative is interviewed between June 1, 1993 and May 31, 1994, 0 otherwise
Interview Yr 3	1 if firm representative is interviewed after May 31, 1994, 0 otherwise
Vacancy Ave	Average months of most recent vacancies at the firm
Sales Last Yr Up	1 if firm sales increased over the past year, 0 otherwise
Sales Last Yr Down	1 if firm sales decreased over the past year, 0 otherwise
Sales Last Yr Same	1 if firm sales were the same as the past year, 0 otherwise
Sales Last Yr Missing	1 if firm did not report sales change over the past year, 0 otherwise
Sales Last 5 Yr Up	1 if firm sales increased over the past 5-10 years, 0 otherwise
Sales Last 5 Yr Down	1 if firm sales decreased over the past 5-10 years, 0 otherwise
Sales Last 5 Yr Same	1 if firm sales were the same as the average over the previous 5-10 years, 0 otherwise
Sales Last 5 Yr Missing	1 if firm did not report what happened to sales over the past 5-10 years, 0 otherwise

*Data Source, Multi-City Telephone Employer Survey (MCTES)

Appendix Table 2: *Probit Estimates of Probability of Firm Offering Employees Health Insurance**

VARIABLES	POOLED DATA		VARIABLES	POOLED DATA	
	Spec A (n=3053)	Spec B (n=2989)		Spec A (n=3053)	Spec B (n=2989)
	Model A (n=3053)	Model B (n=2989)		Model A (n=3053)	Model B (n=2989)
5-9 Employees	.064** (.022)	.062** (.022)	1-9% Clerical Employees	-.039* (.023)	-.042* (.023)
10-19 Employees	.132*** (.016)	.132*** (.016)	Majority Clerical Employees	.029 (.024)	.029 (.022)
20-49 Employees	.164*** (.016)	.164*** (.016)	Missing Clerical Employees	-.028 (.078)	-.039 (.081)
50-99 Employees	.168*** (.014)	.167*** (.014)	No Sales Employees	-.058** (.024)	-.060*** (.024)
100-249 Employees	.207*** (.014)	.207*** (.014)	1-9% Sales Employees	.031 (.026)	.029 (.026)
Greater than 249 Employees	.218*** (.016)	.216*** (.016)	Majority Sales Employees	-.053* (.029)	-.052* (.029)
Part Time Employees	.285 e07 (.465 e07)	.188 e07 (.470 e04)	Missing Sales Employees	.063 (.059)	.059 (.060)
Seasonal Employees	.117 e03 (.114 e03)	.113 e03 (.115 e03)	No Blue Collar Employees	.037 (.023)	.033 (.024)
Temporary Employees	.177 e03 (.264 e03)	.176 e03 (.273 e03)	1-9% Blue Collar Employees	.047 (.030)	.042 (.031)
Contract Employees	.152 e03 (.276 e03)	.148 e03 (.290 e03)	Majority Blue Collar Employees	.002 (.022)	.000 (.022)
Multiple Worksites	-.075*** (.017)	-.073*** (.017)	Missing Blue Collar Employees	-.076 (.066)	-.070 (.066)
Union	.0001 (.0001)	.0001 (.0001)	Atlanta	.041** (.020)	.039* (.020)
For Profit	-.001 (.020)	-.002 (.027)	Boston	.060*** (.018)	.058*** (.019)
Central City	.017 (.017)	.011 (.017)	Detroit	.019 (.025)	.018 (.026)
No H.S. Dropouts	.089*** (.020)	.090*** (.020)	Mining/Agriculture Industry	-.029 (.198)	-.038 (.204)
1-9% H.S. Dropouts	.039 (.026)	.031 (.027)	Construction Industry	.012 (.052)	.003 (.054)
Majority H.S. Dropouts	-.124*** (.040)	-.117*** (.040)	Manufacturing Industry	.084*** (.020)	.077*** (.020)
Missing H.S. Dropout	-.077* (.047)	-.079* (.048)	Transportation Industry	-.058 (.038)	-.061 (.040)
No College Attendance	-.042 (.030)	-.042 (.031)	Whole Sale Trade Industry	.020 (.031)	.009 (.032)
1-9% College Attendance	.031 (.027)	.027 (.027)	Retail Trade Industry	-.099*** (.028)	-.100*** (.029)
Majority College Attendance	-.029 (.020)	-.029 (.020)	Finance Industry	-.031 (.032)	-.037 (.034)
Missing College Attendance	.044 (.030)	.037 (.031)	Public Administration Industry	.049 (.056)	.051 (.055)
No Clerical Employees	-.139*** (.032)	-.138*** (.033)	Missing Industry	.048 (.035)	.045 (.036)

Appendix Table 2: (Continued) *Probit Estimates of Probability of Firm Offering Empl. Health Insurance**

VARIABLES	POOLED DATA Spec A (n=3053) Model A (n=3053)	Spec B (n=2989) Model B (n=2989)
Interview Year 1	.018 (.031)	.017 (.031)
Interview Year 2	.024 (.028)	.021 (.029)
Vacancy Ave		-.004 (.003)
Sales Last Year Up		-.051* (.030)
Sales Last Year Down		-.070** (.038)
Sales Last Year Missing		-.041 (.031)
Sales Last 5 Years Up		.057*** (.022)
Sales Last 5 Years Down		.026 (.027)
Sales Last 5 Years Missing		.033 (.031)
No White Males	-.025 (.025)	-.026 (.025)
1-9% White Male	-.022 (.028)	-.019 (.027)
At Least 50% White Male	.038* (.019)	.042** (.019)
Missing White Male Composition	.134 (.061)	.120 (.071)
No White Females	-.028 (.027)	-.029 (.027)
1-9% White Female	-.022 (.028)	-.017 (.028)
At Least 50% White Female	-.017 (.022)	-.024 (.022)
Missing White Female Composition	-.094 (.133)	-.049 (.132)
F-Tests for Combined Male and Female Subcategories		
No White Male and No White Female	2.82* [0.093]	3.01* [0.083]
1-9 % White Male and 1-9% White Female	1.65 [0.200]	1.08 [0.299]
At Least 50% White Male and at Least 50% White Female	0.50 [0.479]	0.38 [0.537]
F-Tests for Gender Difference		
No White Male vs. No White Female	0.01 [0.931]	0.01 [0.942]

VARIABLES	POOLED DATA Spec A (n=3053) Model A (n=3053)	Spec B (n=2989) Model B (n=2989)
1-9 % White Male vs. 1-9% White Female	0.00 [0.998]	0.00 [0.971]
At Least 50% White Male vs At Least 50% White Female	4.28** [0.039]	5.97** [0.015]
Chi Square Stat	720***	719***
Pseudo R2	.22	.23

*Notes: Columns report marginal probit estimates evaluated at mean values for all the included variables of the likelihood of firms offering insurance to the last employee hired, standard errors are reported in parentheses. Spec A is our preferred model, while Spec B contains some variables that might be endogenous such as firm performance in the past year and over a longer span of time. The "White Model" controls for composition of white employees at the firm while the "Nonwhite Model" controls for composition of black and Latino employees at the firm.

VII. Broadband Matters to All of Us

REY RAMSEY, J.D.

Fifty-four percent. That's the number of African Americans who don't have broadband according to a new report from the U.S. Department of Commerce.[1]

Why is that number important, you may ask? Simply put, having more of our fellow citizens gain access to technology and the Internet is critically important to helping create the cutting edge ideas which create jobs and opportunity.

We can do better. Today, more than 100 million Americans don't have broadband at home, including millions of African Americans.[2] The Commerce Department also reports that African Americans in rural areas had lower levels of broadband use (29 percent) than that of urban areas (48 percent).[3]

Wider adoption of broadband is one of the best fiscal stimulus policies we can make as a nation because new industries, companies and jobs are created as a result. One study showed that just a 7 percent increase in adoption could grow well over one million jobs.[4] At the same time, greater deployment of broadband will enable all of our citizens to more fully participate in our economy as many of the jobs of tomorrow and training programs will be done from home.

Blair Levin, the leader of the Obama Administration's Omnibus Broadband Initiative, recently spoke about the amazing benefits broadband can bring to all of our citizens, especially our most vulnerable and those most in need of a friendly hand to help them reach up the economic ladder.

"Over the last thirty years, we have seen increases in income inequality, residential segregation and social isolation, and the concentration of disadvantage," said Mr. Levin. "The number of neighborhoods today with a dangerous poverty rate—poverty above 30%—is higher than it was in 2000. In areas with a dense concentration of poverty, jobs disappear. Opportunity disappears. The American tradition of justice, of achieving the American dream, emphasizes equality of opportunity—of having access to equal sets of resources that can enable us, our families, our children to succeed. Let me be clear: access to high-speed Internet, even when paired with the digital skills needed to use it, is not a guarantee of such opportunity—it also requires values such as hard work and diligence that neither technology nor government can provide. But broadband can help people get access to better jobs, better education, better health care information and improved government services."[5]

He's exactly right. Connecting people to information and the Internet can deliver real results and greater opportunity. In effect, as John Chambers, the Chairman and CEO of Cisco and one of the founding members of TechNet says, "broadband and the Internet fundamentally can improve the way we live, play, learn and work."

For so many of our young people, more broadband means greater virtual access to better educational opportunities. Distance learning enabled by rich broadband can give America's students—including millions of African American youngsters—access to coursework they may not be able to receive in their schools and thus improved learning. What's more, 70 percent of America's young people do homework with the help of Internet resources—putting those without access at a serious disadvantage.

More broadband also holds the capacity to improve our health. Today, we have the capacity to link an 88 year old grandmother from rural Mississippi who is unable to get out of her house to a needed doctor or specialists miles away for a "virtual house call" via the Internet. Monitoring technology enabled through broadband can also allow our elderly citizens to live longer in their homes and delay having to move to an elder care facility. This can bring not only improved quality of life, but real cost savings. Furthermore, if we adopt information technology tools through broadband on a wider scale in just a few years, think about the positive health outcomes that will result.

Broadband also equals jobs and opportunity for African Americans. Even though the nation saw our unemployment rate recently tick down from

10 percent to 9.7 percent in January, joblessness in the African-American community rose to an unacceptable 16.5 percent.[6] That's roughly double the amount of white unemployment at 8.7 percent.[7] In many of our major urban areas, unemployment of African American men rises above a staggering 20 percent.[8]

...getting these policies right will help create millions of needed family wage jobs...

Technology jobs pay on average 40 percent more than other jobs in our economy.[9] Thus if more of us have proper access and training (often just basic computer skills) we can provide a boost up the economic ladder. Most jobs today are posted online and are not necessarily posted in local newspapers. Without access to the Internet, finding those jobs is more difficult and training people for these skills thus becomes critically important.

Without greater Internet access in many African-American communities, the sad fact is that we may actually be increasing inequality. Working online helps you make more money. Searching for jobs online links you to more opportunity. Learning online speeds your educational opportunities. But for those not online, the gap between technology rich and poor only widens unless we do more.

Our public policies matter when it comes to expanding opportunity through broadband connectivity. One Economy, a nonprofit I

founded in 2000, launched the Bring IT Home campaign, a bipartisan effort supported by a diverse group of technology companies, Internet Service Providers, and nonprofit organizations, to change the way states allocate low-income housing tax credits to encourage the availability of broadband in low-income housing. Forty-two states changed their policies and broadband was brought into the homes of over 300,000 low-income Americans as a result.

Recently, the Obama Administration—through the Federal Communications Commission—unveiled its national broadband plan. This represents smart policy. Until this effort came about, the United States was the only major country without a strategic broadband plan.[10] The goal of putting broadband in 100 million homes with speeds of over 100 megabits per seconds matters as new innovation and job creation will result. From where I sit as a representative of America's high tech sector, we have made strides in the past few years in increasing the broadband footprint but it's not enough as our global competitors are aggressively mapping out their digital futures because they realize economic growth is linked directly to strong innovation leadership.

Broadband (and the higher speeds and innovation that come with it) could transform public safety by enabling an interoperable network that would allow our first-responders to communicate effectively in times of crisis. It could transform our energy use by enabling a Smart Grid and lowering our energy bills. It could transform health care, lowering costs for all Americans by enabling telemedicine, remote monitoring, and more use of electronic health records. And more broadband access will no doubt improve educational opportunities, training and job creation for African Americans.

Our nation's history favors a strong public-private roadmap. In earlier generations, Americans made sure that communications platforms like telephony, radio and TV became ubiquitous services and drivers of innovation, jobs, and growth in the economy through a combination of private investment, targeted public investments and thoughtful public policies. And just a few decades ago, the Internet itself derived from a thoughtful partnership between the Department of Defense, research institutions and private industry.

We look forward to continue working with the Administration on this important broadband roadmap. In last year's economic stimulus, we made historic investments to spur more broadband. We must keep this momentum going. America has always grown our economy through disruptive technologies that create jobs and a better quality of life.

With quality implementation of a new broadband roadmap, we have the potential to make broadband affordable, available and adopted throughout the nation.

In the end, getting these policies right will help create millions of needed family wage jobs at a time when our country—and so many of our fellow African-American citizens—needs them the most.

NOTES

[1] DIGITAL NATION: 21st Century America's Progress Towards Universal Broadband Internet Access: US Dept of Commerce/NTIA's report on U.S. broadband Internet connectivity based on a survey of over 50,000 households commissioned by NTIA and conducted by the United States Census Bureau. February 16, 2010.

[2] Oped by FCC Chairman Genachowski, *http://www.huffingtonpost. com/julius-genachowski/americas-2020-broadband-v_b_467234. html,* February 18, 2010.

[3] DIGITAL NATION: 21st Century America's Progress Towards Universal Broadband Internet Access: US Dept of Commerce/NTIA's report on U.S. broadband Internet connectivity based on a survey of over 50,000 households commissioned by NTIA and conducted by the United States Census Bureau. February 16, 2010.

[4] Connected Nation, "The Economic Impact Of Stimulating Broadband Nationally," Executive Summary, 2/21/08.

[5] Speech by Blair Levin, Executive Director, Omnibus Broadband Initiative, at the Minority Media and Telecommunications Council's Broadband and Social Justice Summit, January 22, 2010.

[6] Seattle Medium, Black Leaders Finally Meet With Obama on Jobs by Pharoh Martin NNPA National Correspondent 2/17/2010 based on BLS Statistics *http://www.seattlemedium.com/News/article/article.as p?NewsID=101443&sID=3&ItemSource=L*

[7] Black Star News, "Obama Responds To Dire Urban America Conditions" Article By Marc H. Morial President Urban League, February 18th, 2010.

[8] Black Star News, "Obama Responds To Dire Urban America Conditions" Article By Marc H. Morial President Urban League, February 18th, 2010.

[9] Speech by Blair Levin, Executive Director, Omnibus Broadband Initiative, at the Minority Media and Telecommunications Council's Broadband and Social Justice Summit, January 22, 2010.

[10] Reuters, "US to unveil broadband plan Mar 17, sees barriers" Feb 23, 2010, By John Poirier.

VIII. The Philadelphia Story: Small Business Growth = Job Creation

PATRICIA A. COULTER, M.ED.

Minority entrepreneurship, at first blush, may not seem synonymous to the creation of new jobs, however given that minority businesses are forming at a faster rate than overall businesses and entrepreneurship is responsible for most newly created jobs in the U.S., minority business growth offers unique solutions to America's job crisis, while building economic equity and developing communities.

This essay examines how the execution of a community based model to grow small minority businesses can in turn create more jobs in urban areas. While it is but one example, our experience in Philadelphia, where the Urban League of Philadelphia launched its Urban League Entrepreneurship Center one year ago, can be instructive on how to utilize the small business market to fuel job creation in our country.

Growing minority businesses is no easy feat. According to James H. Lowry, minority businesses often lack the size and capacity that majority businesses have. In addition, they are disproportionately crowded into low-growth and no-growth sectors and their capital is based on personal debt and family financing rather than business loans, equity and other capital market resources.[1] Lowry advises that, in order to close the gap, "all of the major players in the field—large corporations, government officials, and minority entrepreneurs—[must] shift their mindset to focus on six strategic imperatives:

» *First, they must think differently, and strategically about minority business development;*

» *Second, they must develop large minority businesses with strong capabilities;*

» *Third, they must collaborate on ways to develop minority businesses of size;*

» *Fourth, they must use emerging domestic markets as growth engines;*

» *Fifth, they must globalize minority businesses;*

» *Sixth, they must embrace innovative strategies for financing the growth of minority businesses.*[2]

An example of one minority-owned business that is making the leap to scale is PRWT Services, Inc., a minority-owned business that over the last 20 years has strategically put down roots and planted itself as a major business in the country. PRWT Services, Inc. is a national, diversified enterprise operating in pharmaceutical manufacturing and distribution, facilities management and maintenance businesses headquartered in the Greater Philadelphia Region. Founded in

1988, PRWT is certified minority business enterprise with the National Minority Supplier Development Council. It has been ranked in the Top 100 Minority-Owned Businesses in America by *Black Enterprise* magazine for the past eight years and earning the publication's endorsement as Company of the Year in 2009. This after the company, through its wholly-owned subsidiary Cherokee Pharmaceuticals acquired a manufacturing facility from Merck & Co. With the creation of Cherokee and the acquisition, PRWT became the first minority-owned manufacturer of Active Pharmaceutical Ingredients (API's) in the United States.

According to Harold T. Epps, president & CEO, "PRWT is ok with being the *first* minority-owned company to grow to this level of scale in the Greater Philadelphia Region but we don't want to be the *only* one to get there."

By opening an entrepreneurship center in Philadelphia, ULP hopes to facilitate the path for minority businesses and contribute to the economic growth of the region. Philadelphia's Black businesses take in annual receipts of $83,000, compared to $139,000 for Hispanic businesses and $256,000 for Asian businesses.[3] *The State of Black Philadelphia* reports that the rate of Black business ownership is 50% that of Whites.[4] Furthermore, *Everyone's Business: Building Minority Businesses to Scale* reports that "in a comparison of eight other regions, Philadelphia's minority-owned firms [all minorities] have the smallest average employment size (36 total employees). Only five Philadelphia minority-owned firms have more than 50 employees, and just one has more than 200 employees." Philadelphia's businesses also report lower net profits per employee, and as a result they have a harder time growing to scale.[5]

The Urban League's Entrepreneurship Center will focus on helping African-American owned businesses grow to scale so that they can have greater market presence, increase revenues and create additional jobs for the region. Through this program we consult, coach and encourage businesses owners to expand their thinking, knowledge and experience. We provide technical assistance, networking opportunities and linkages to financial, management and legal resources for these emerging businesses. We also assist businesses to reorganize and restructure to achieve efficient, effective and productive delivery of their product or service to its customer base and their new markets. All of these services are offered through both training in group sessions as well as one-on-one consulting.

Target Market

The Urban League of Philadelphia primarily focuses on African-American businesses that gross revenues between $50,000 – $500,000 dollars annually. We offer a tiered level of services based on a company size, years of experience and gross revenues. This allows us to better match these businesses with the right coach/consultant. The companies have a local presence in the Philadelphia metropolitan area. This includes the surrounding counties (Bucks, Chester, Delaware & Montgomery) along with Wilmington, DE and Camden County, NJ.

Our secondary market focuses on businesses that have gross revenues of more than $500,000 dollars annually. Again, we provide services in a tiered format to ensure that companies

of similar experience and size are grouped together in workshops.

Finally, we focus on aspiring African-American entrepreneurs to create a linkage between them and industry opportunities through training. We encourage entrepreneurs to pursue opportunities in growth markets and emerging industries where traditionally there is a lack of African-American presence.

> ...focus on helping African-American owned businesses grow to scale so that they can have greater market presence, increase revenues and create additional jobs for the region.

Intake Process

Our service delivery begins when the potential client either calls or walks through our office doors for information. The ULEC Coordinator is typically the first point of contact for all patrons that contact us. There is an inquiry about the type of business support needed and desired and an intake packet is completed. Once the intake process is finished we link the client to a business coach to conduct the assessment process. After that the next step could be a workshop or it can be one-on-one consulting sessions. The ULEC provides individual sessions and conduct group sessions and workshops around specific business topics. Lastly, the consultant develops an action plan with the entrepreneur or business owner to begin implementation.

Assessment Tools/ Progress Tracking

As a part of the intake process we utilize a web-based self assessment tool that allows for client tracking and management to track the evolution of businesses as they move along the mentoring and coaching continuum. The system is used for maintaining client data, reporting, monitoring trends and tracking workflow.

Coaches/Consultants

The Urban League has developed a pool of coaches and consultants who are matched with clients based on their expertise and the client's needs as outlined during the intake process. Coaches primarily provide advice and counsel to clients, Consultants hold them accountable for results to improve their business. Consultants must have a minimum of 3 years of business consulting experience in a specialty field:

» *Accounting*
» *Advertising/Copywriting*
» *Business Plan Preparation*
» *Cash Flow Management*
» *Environmental Issues*
» *Exporting*
» *Financial Management*
» *Government Procurement*
» *Government Regulations*
» *Graphic Design*

» *Insurance*
» *Intellectual Property*
» *International Trade*
» *Legal Issues*
» *Loan Packages*
» *Marketing*
» *Market Research*
» *Personnel Management*
» *Product Development*
» *Sales*
» *Technology Commercialization*

Workshops

Networking and building relationships are key components to a small businesses growth strategy. Through the Urban League Entrepreneurship Center model, relationships are forged when minority business owners meet together at many of the workshops presented by business experts. These sessions are held weekly either in the evenings, or during lunch at what we call "brown bag lunch series." Our average attendance at these sessions is 40-50 persons per month. A sampling of the workshops and "brown bag" series are:

» *Prospecting Techniques for Small Businesses*
» *Crafting a Winning Positioning Statement*
» *Create a Winning Marketing Statement to Keep People Talking About You*
» *Generating Leads Through Technology*
» *Maintaining Customer Loyalty*
» *Women in charge-Leadership, Vision and Growth*
» *The Talent Pool is Full—Hiring the Right Employees*
» *Five People You Need to Meet to Help Grow Your Business*

» *Becoming a Dynamic Salesperson*

» *Are You Loan Ready*

» *Unleashing the Power of Us!*

» *Turner School of Construction Management*

» *What Does Your Brand Say About You?*

» *The Power of Partnerships*

» *Learning to Network—Session 1*

» *Learning to Network—Session 2*

» *How to Grow Your Business in 90 Days*

» *Start Your Own Business Now*

» *The Power of Having a Plan of Action*

Strategic Relationships

Strategic partnerships are extremely important to our ability to serve all segments of the community through entrepreneurship. We realize that this venture and our service delivery will not be based on being all things to all businesses. So, it is vital to identify organizations with similar objectives and goals to meet the economic needs of the African-American entrepreneur through business support and education.

This relationship with other agencies and with the local business community is a key component to ULP having a strong support network for the entrepreneurs and businesses that we serve. The Strategic partner must have a proven track record in providing quality technical assistance and education to small business in the African-American community. An example of a strategic business relationship is the one the Urban League has with the Greater Philadelphia Chamber of Commerce who launched last year its CEO Access Network, a Mentor Protégé Program that pairs

business leaders with operators of smaller minority-owned companies. The initiative, in its second year, is part of an agenda to bring greater diversity to chamber operations and help minority-owned businesses grow. The program included 11 pairings in first year and is expected to expand to 20 in its second year. Likewise, the City of Philadelphia, through its Office of Economic Opportunity, which now resides in the Commerce Department, a strategic move by the Mayor, has set a goal to increase its M/W/DSBE participation from 17.8% in FY2008 to 25% by the end of FY2011. According to OEO's strategic plan, "the universe of economic opportunities being considered need no longer be limited solely to "City Contracts,...the Administration can take a more comprehensive approach to both entrepreneurship and employment opportunities and broaden the discussion of diversity and inclusion to a regional and even global stage." [6]

After just one year, the ULP is working with over 100 small businesses utilizing this model. Salon Tenshi, a beauty products based company, came to the Urban League in January 2009 shortly after their salon grand opening, with two employees and revenues of $120,000. After the intake and assessment stages they were assigned a consultant who assisted them with a growth strategy. The owners were also paired with a consultant to help strengthen their strategic planning and operations. In just the one year Salon Tenshi's revenues now exceed $200,000, seven employees, and a new product line.

Natural Pest Control engaged the services of the Urban League. The founder and president had been running the business for over 30 years with revenues at $500,000 and 8 employees. It was clear he needed a marketing strategy. His Coach advised he take advantage of several training workshops, including the E200 series co-sponsored with the SBA. Natural Pest Control's today is looking to hire 4 additional technicians and support services representatives after being awarded a multi-million-dollar contract that will increase revenues to $3,000,000. His consultants, a financial management, operations, strategy planning experts all worked closely to help him align his business practices with sales, technology and procurement opportunities.

Conclusion

The business owners have used their success to empower others. They have as an example right here in Philadelphia, PRWT Services, Inc., which grew from a start-up in 1988 to a company bringing in $167,000,000 in just 20 years later and employing 1,500 people. (*Black Enterprise* May 2009). There's a PRWT Services, Inc. out there in every community. A small business yearning to get access to capital and talent, ready to demonstrate its ability to provide quality services and eager to pay it forward and bring others along.

While these minority-owned businesses, like Salon Tenshi and Natural Pest Control, are not yet on the same scale as PRWT Services, Inc., they know they can help make a difference and bring resources to their communities. Minority-owned businesses, whether major players in the game like PRWT Services, Inc., or emerging leaders like Salon Tenshi and Natural Pest Control, want what we all want

and need to see happen—small business growth and the creation of jobs for all.

REFERENCES

Black Enterprise magazine, *Top 100 Black Businesses*, May, 2009.

Boston Consulting Group, James H. Lowry, *Realizing the New Agenda for Minority Business Development*, November 2005.

Economy League Greater Philadelphia, Review, Spring 2008, *Everyone's Business: Building Minority Businesses to Scale.*

Friedman, Thomas L., "More (Steve) Jobs, Jobs, Jobs, Jobs," *The New York Times*, Sunday Opinion, January 24, 2010.

Klein, Karen E. "Minority Start-Ups: A Measure of Progress." *Business Week*. August 25, 2005.

Merritt, Athena D. "Philadelphia Included by SBA in effort to spur growth." Philadelphia Business Journal, March 28, 2008.

Office of Economic Opportunity, City of Philadelphia Department of Commerce, *Philly Works: Economic Opportunity Strategic Plan*, February, 2010.

Policy Link. "Minority Contracting."2005; *http://www.policylink.org/ EDTK/Minority Contracting/default.html.*

The State of Black Philadelphia, 2007, Economics Index

U.S. Census Survey of Business Owners, 2002.

NOTES

[1] Boston Consulting Group, *Realizing the New Agenda for Minority Business Development.*

[2] Ibid

[3] Survey of Business Owners, U.S. Census 2002.

[4] Urban League of Philadelphia, *The State of Black Philadelphia, 2007.*

[5] Economy League of Greater Philadelphia, "Everyone's Business: Building Minority Businesses to Scale," Greater Philadelphia Regional Review, Spring 2008.

[6] Office of Economic Opportunity, City of Philadelphia Department of Commerce, Economic Opportunity Strategic Plan, February 2010.

IX. Opening New Doors Through Volunteerism

BARTON J. TAYLOR, M.P.A.

In today's economy, many would say just having gainful employment should be enough to be grateful for. However, you have to be strategic about your career and think about your tomorrow, just like the companies and organizations do. How are you being prepared for it? Are you being developed or denied growth? With a bad economy, one of the first things to get reduced or eradicated is professional development.

So how do you obtain skills that will benefit you, your professional development and current and future employers? One answer that is commonly overlooked is volunteerism.

Volunteering is the practice of people working on behalf of others or a particular cause without payment for their time and services.[1]

Volunteering promotes good or improved human quality of life, but people also volunteer for their own skill development, to meet others, to make contacts for possible employment, or to have fun.[2] The skill development component is the area of focus on during this discussion. Volunteering can be the difference between the corner cubicle and the corner suite.

Current Job Market

We're experiencing an economic recession that has not been felt since the Great Depression. Companies have been either financially collapsing or cutting back to the bare bones just to stay afloat. The US economy lost 2.8 million jobs in 2008 alone.[3] At the end of 2009, over 15 million Americans were unemployed and African Americans spiked the jobless odometer at 16.7 percent.[4] The sectors that lost the most jobs in this current recession—besides the financial sector—are construction, retail, and manufacturing, as well as hospitality and transportation. In fact, government, a sector once immune to such recessions, has faced some alarming reductions.

Doing more with less is no longer a management buzz phrase but now the order of the day. Part of doing more with less is investing less in talent development. It is predicted that personnel will now have to be self-developed or find alternative means to broaden their professional development. Even as the recession begins to show signs of slowing job losses, it still should be realized that job competition will be greater than in recent memory.

How can you distinguish yourself from the job competition if your employer is not providing development opportunities? Your answer lies in your ability to give more of yourself to something worth receiving it—through volunteerism.

In any job market, job opportunities are gained in one of two ways—cold acquisition or hot referrals. Cold acquisition is when you look at advertised positions and make inquiries, get screened and (hopefully) get an interview and possible offer. The hot referral is when someone on the inside or connected to the inside refers you to that advertised position or to the non-public job opportunities. This is achieved through networking, having people see your work, value and skills in other settings. These opportunities rarely find their way to a job portal or the want ads. Based on this, coupled with the fact that current employers are offering less professional development opportunities, how can you gain the skills and experience needed, while simultaneously positioning yourself for that fateful moment of networking into an unknown job opportunity? Volunteerism is the answer.

Volunteering promotes good or improved human quality of life.

The State of Volunteerism

In his 1961 Inaugural Address, President Kennedy challenged Americans to ask not what your country can do for you, but what you can do for your country. From these words the Peace Corps was formed. Fast forward forty-eight years later to 2009 when President Obama challenged us to serve the cause that is America. Both asked that people give of themselves to causes, issues or problems that would benefit from their talents, skills and determination. Volunteerism then and now is still strong and relevant. According to the Corporation for National & Community Service the current state of volunteerism is:

» *Over 61.8 million Americans volunteered 8 billion hours in 2008.[5]*

» *The center's preliminary report states that the economic recession has not had an adverse impact on volunteerism in the US.*

» *As the economy slows and nonprofit organizations struggle to provide services on smaller budgets, volunteers become even more vital to the health of our nation's communities.*

» *Between September 2008 and March 2009, more than a third (37%) of nonprofit organizations report increasing the number of volunteers they use, and almost half (48%) foresee increasing their usage of volunteers in the coming year.[6]*

» *Volunteers were much more likely than non-volunteers to donate to a charitable cause in 2008, with 78.2 percent contributing $25 or more compared to 38.5 percent of non-volunteers.[7]*

Although this is a good prognosis of volunteerism, there are still some challenges that need to be addressed. The main cancer to volunteerism is What's in it for Me? This has always existed but was disguised because it was taboo to expose any hidden agendas in your volunteer activities. Today's volunteers bring these agendas to the forefront. More and more organizations are having to answer this question or begin to feel the exodus of volunteers who are seeking outlets that can answer this need. The problem with this is that the volunteer is possibly missing out on possible career changing opportunities in

search of a fast answer or instant gratification. The other side of this coin is you get what you give and those that give little receive even less. In the job market, it's partly who you know that gets you the dough. If you're never around to make contacts, showcase your skills, talents and dedication, how can you make that network work for you? This is the hidden treasure that those seeking fast gratification miss. They miss the value of volunteering. The value of volunteering in terms of jobs can be categorized into the following reimbursements for time, energy and expertise given to a cause:

» *Supplemental Skills Development*

» *Broadening Personal & Professional Networks*

» *Confidence Boosting*

These value centers are the core of what I call *Professional Re-Tooling through Volunteerism.*

Re-Tooling Your Keys

When a door of greater professional opportunity is closed, how do you open it? Many of us possess keys but it may not have the right key so a re-tooling is in order. One way to re-tool your key is through volunteerism. Volunteering allows you to spread your wings into areas that may not be available professionally through supplemental skills development. For example, someone who has been trying to become a project lead at their job but lacks certain skill sets to be chosen can build expertise in that area by volunteering as project or program leads. Someone who lacks financial management skills can volunteer as treasurer or auditor with a community organization to get that experience. Some may even work in a company that is lacking diversity, so they volunteer with an organization that deals with diversity issues. Volunteerism allows you to be exposed to opportunities to re-tool your skills while minimizing the risk involved, i.e. being fired.

Volunteering also broadens your personal and professional networks. If you ask hiring executives to identity the main factor they consider in hiring, a majority would probably respond "familiarity with the applicant and their work." People are more comfortable with people they know. Volunteering puts you in position to meet more people from all areas of the community-business, non-profit and government. This is working to make your network work for you.

> # Volunteerism allows you to be exposed to opportunities to re-tool your skills while minimizing the risk involved...

Last, volunteering can boost your confidence in your skills and abilities. Many volunteers grow in their roles and soon become more and more adept in their volunteer activities as team leads, project directors even leading the volunteer apparatus itself. I witness this confidence boosting phenomenon frequently in the National Urban League Young Professionals, the National Urban League's auxiliary of 21-40

year olds. Members in chapters all across the country build confidence in their abilities to change their communities and lives all while volunteering with their local Urban League affiliates. I can even attribute my skill development, growth and confidence through volunteering. Other professional success stories that volunteering contributed to include:

» *An Urban League Young Professional volunteer gained experience in marketing, event planning and team management, which has directly contributed in three promotions including a senior level position.*

» *An Urban League volunteer led that local Urban League's young professionals volunteer auxiliary, gaining valuable organization and fundraising skills, which contributed to that volunteer being chosen as President and CEO of that same local Urban League a few years later.*

» *A volunteer at a National Urban League event met a business owner who noticed how hard this volunteer was working. After a few conversations and follow up meetings, this volunteer was hired to head this business sales apparatus.*

The ability to learn transferable skills and the confidence to execute those skills is one of the many benefits of volunteering. These opportunities are realized because of the effort given by those volunteering who took advantage of the opportunities that volunteering presents.

Conclusion

Many may read this and conclude that I'm advocating that you go into volunteering with other agendas. This would be an incorrect assumption. Instead, what I want you to conclude is that opportunity knocks whenever and wherever and those that are prepared for it will be able to hear and answer the knock.

I want you to conclude that volunteering is a win-win activity where you can give and receive because your intent was genuine and that unselfish actions lead to unselfish rewards. More important, I want you to conclude that in a good or bad job market, volunteering can be that difference between good and great, between barely succeeding and succeeding beyond expectations.

NOTES

1 Volunteering. March 1, 2008. *http://en.wikipedia.org/wiki/ Volunteering (accessed February 14, 2010).*

2 Ibid

3 Goldman, David. Special Report. January 9, 2009. *http://money. cnn.com/2009/01/09/news/economy/jobs_december/* (accessed February 10, 2010).

4 National Urban League Policy Institute, December 2009 Jobs Report, January 9, 2010. *http://www.nul.org/sites/default/files/2009%20 December%20Employment%20Report.pdf* (accessed February 11, 2010).

5 Corporation for National & Community Service. *VolunteeringinAmerica.gov.* July 2009. *http:// www.volunteeringinamerica.gov/assets/resources/ VolunteeringInAmericaResearchHighlights.pdf* (accessed February 2, 2010).

6 Ibid

7 Ibid

A Call to Action

STEPHANIE J. JONES, J.D.
NATIONAL URBAN LEAGUE POLICY INSTITUTE

Support the strong, give courage to the timid,
remind the indifferent, and warn the opposed...
  - Whitney M. Young, Jr.

As the National Urban League celebrates our Centennial this year, we are taking the time to reflect on our history and how it shapes, informs and inspires the work we continue into our second century.

An important part of that work is *The State of Black America*, which educates, motivates, and challenges our communities, the public, government officials, and political leaders on issues important to African Americans, including economic empowerment, housing, education, civil rights and social justice. In this year's edition, we again tackle all of these concerns—this time, within the framework of the overarching issue of our time: the unemployment crisis.

As we unequivocally document in the foregoing chapters, the unemployment crisis poses an extraordinary challenge unlike any we've seen in decades. It requires our unwavering and fierce focus and smart, immediate action if we are to keep the crisis from festering into a national disaster.

This issue of *The State of Black America* shines a bright light on the unemployment crisis and offers dynamic, well-thought-out solutions, based on our 100 years of experience, for how to pull this nation back from the brink of an unemployment catastrophe and put us back on the track of full economic empowerment and security for all.

In the 34 years since the first issue of *The State of Black America* was published in 1976, this nation has seen much change and much progress. Black Americans have substantially increased our political and economic power. But even though we have come far, some things, sadly, remain the same.

For example, the first *State of Black America* reported that, in 1974, the median income for black families was $7,808 compared with a median income for white families of $13,356—an Equality Index of 58.5. Today, *The State of Black America 2010* Equality Index for median income is 62%—a mere four points of progress in 35 years.

Black unemployment in 1975 was 14.1 percent, compared with white unemployment of 7.6 percent. Thirty-four years later, *The State of Black America 2010* reports that in 2009, black unemployment was 14.8 percent compared with a white unemployment rate of 8.5 percent—rates that have not been seen in this country in decades. We are backsliding. Drastic action is required.

This year's *The State of Black America* offers solid data, analysis and recommendations designed to stem this regression and put this nation and our urban communities on track to full economic opportunity, empowerment and strength. Many of these recommendations are directed to our elected officials who are in positions to create and implement public policies that have tremendous impact on our communities. We call upon these elected officials to step up and do the right thing. But the responsibility is not theirs alone. We have a duty to hold them accountable by engaging, pressuring and insisting upon accountability from our representatives—from the President to Congress to state elected officials to our local mayors, school boards, and county commissions and community. Demanding accountability is not a privilege reserved for the well-wired, well-financed few; it is a right guaranteed by our citizenship and cemented with our votes.

But our responsibility goes beyond exacting accountability from our government officials. We—*all of us*—have a duty to do everything in our power to educate our children, increase our financial literacy, build personal and collective economic security and create healthier communities.

The State of Black America 2010 is a potent and invaluable tool that all of us can use to achieve these goals. The information contained on these pages can empower us to carry out Whitney Young's charge to *support the strong, give courage to the timid, remind the indifferent and warn the opposed.* Inspired by our history, armed with knowledge, and committed to progress, let us now move forward together into our next century—renewed, committed and equipped to ensuring that the state of Black America is strong, secure, prosperous and whole.

About the Authors

Bernard E. Anderson, Ph.D.

Dr. Bernard E. Anderson is the former Whitney M. Young Professor of Management in the Wharton School of the University of Pennsylvania. An expert on labor economics and human resource management, Dr. Anderson is a former Assistant Secretary of the U.S. Department of Labor for the Employment Standards Administration. He chairs the National Urban League President's Council of Economic Advisers.

Terry Clark

Terry Clark is the Vice President of Entrepreneurship and Business Development at the National Urban League. He is responsible for the management and oversight of the Entrepreneurship Center which provides management consulting and training services to over 8,000 business owners annually. He is also responsible for the development and assessment of New Market Tax Credit investments through a strategic alliance between Stonehenge Capital and the National Urban League.

Patricia A. Coulter, M.ED.

Patricia A. Coulter is the President and CEO of the Urban League of Philadelphia, where she has served since 2002. Ms. Coulter's background includes general management, business development, executive coaching, management development and college administration. Prior to joining the Urban League, she was Senior Vice President for a Philadelphia-based executive search firm, and Senior Vice President and General Manager at a global career management firm.

William Darity Jr., Ph.D.

Dr. William Darity Jr. is Arts and Sciences Professor of Public Policy Studies, African and African American Studies, and Economics at Duke University and Professor Emeritus of Economics and Sociology at the University of North Carolina at Chapel Hill. He has published more than 200 articles in professional journals spanning the fields of economics, public health, sociology, history, literary criticism, and anthropology. He also has authored or edited 10 books, including lead editorship of the most recent edition of the International Encyclopedia of the Social Sciences (2008). His current research in population studies includes ongoing work on the role of physical appearance—particularly skin shade—on life outcomes ranging from employment to marriage to social disconnectedness to health and wellness.

Education Secretary Arne Duncan

Secretary Arne Duncan, under the leadership of President Obama, is the current U.S. Secretary of Education. Prior to his appointment as secretary of education, Duncan served as the chief executive officer of the Chicago Public Schools, a position to which he was appointed by Mayor Richard M. Daley, from June 2001 through December 2008, becoming the longest-serving big-city education superintendent in the country.

Lance Freeman, Ph.D.

Dr. Lance Freeman is an Associate Professor in the Urban Planning program at Columbia University in New York City. His research focuses on affordable housing, gentrification, ethnic and racial stratification in housing markets, and the relationship between the built environment and well being. Dr. Freeman also has professional experience working as a City Planner for the New York City Housing Authority, and as a budget analyst for the New York City Department of Environmental Protection.

Arthur H. Goldsmith, Ph.D.

Dr. Arthur H. Goldsmith is the *Jackson T. Stephens Professor* of Economics at Washington and Lee University. His research combines insights from economics, psychology, sociology, and history to explore questions regarding wages, employment, unemployment, psychological well-being, access to health-care, and educational accumulation. He has published articles in a number of the professions leading journals including: the *Journal of Economic Literature*, the *Journal of Economic Perspectives*, the *Journal of Human Resources, Economic Inquiry*, the *Southern Economic Journal*, the *Journal of Economic Behavior and Organization*. Grants from *The National Science Foundation* and the *Robert Wood Johnson Foundation* have supported his work in recent years. Professor Goldsmith serves on the editorial board of both the *Journal of Economic Psychology*, and the *Journal of Socio-Economic*.

Darrick Hamilton, Ph.D.

Dr. Darrick Hamilton is an Assistant Professor at Milano—The New School for Management and Urban Policy, an affiliated faculty member in the Department of Economics at The New School for Social Research, an affiliate scholar at the Center for American Progress, and a Co-Associate Director of the American Education Association Summer Research and Minority Scholarship Program. Dr. Hamilton's work focuses on the causes and consequences of racial and ethnic inequality in economic and health outcomes, and he has published articles on disparities in wealth, homeownership, and labor market outcomes.

Stephanie J. Jones, J.D.

Stephanie Jones is the Executive Director of the National Urban League Policy Institute and Editor-in-Chief of *The State of Black America*. She previously served as chief counsel to former North Carolina Sen. John Edwards and Chief of Staff to Rep. Stephanie Tubbs Jones. She is the creator and author of *Sunday Morning Apartheid: A Diversity Study of the Sunday Morning Talk Shows*.

Marc H. Morial

Marc H. Morial is President and CEO of the National Urban League. Since taking the helm in 2003, he has been the primary catalyst for an era of change—a transformation for the 100 year-old civil rights organization. His energetic and skilled leadership has expanded the League's work around an Empowerment agenda, which is redefining civil rights in the 21st century with a renewed emphasis on closing the economic gaps. Under his stewardship the League has expanded its programs, used technology to serve more people and has had record fundraising success towards a 250MM, five year fundraising goal while securing the BBB nonprofit certification, which has established the organization as a leading national nonprofit. In a distinguished professional career that has spanned 25 years as an entrepreneur, lawyer, professor, legislator, President of U.S. Conference of Mayors and two-term Mayor of New Orleans, Marc H. Morial is one of the most accomplished servant-leaders in the nation.

Demetra Smith Nightingale, Ph.D.

Dr. Demetra Smith Nightingale serves on the faculty of the Institute for Policy Studies at Johns Hopkins University, where she teaches graduate courses in Social Policy and in Program Evaluation. Her research includes a number of studies of welfare reform and workforce development; program performance measurement; evaluations of programs for low-income youth, families, and adults; research on the labor market, occupations, and the workplace; and analysis of anti-poverty strategies and programs.

Rey Ramsey, J.D.

Rey Ramsey is President & Chief Executive Officer of TechNet. TechNet is the preeminent bipartisan political network of Chief Executive Officers and Senior Executives of leading U.S. technology companies. Mr. Ramsey is also the Chairman of One Economy, a nonprofit organization devoted to maximizing the potential of technology to help low-income people improve their lives and enter the economic mainstream.

Cy Richardson

Cy Richardson is Vice President of Housing and Community Development at the National Urban League. He is responsible for programs and policies which promote wealth building and asset preservation. He earned his undergraduate degree from the University of North Carolina and holds graduate degrees in urban planning and political science from Pratt Institute and the City University of New York Graduate Center.

Labor Secretary Hilda L. Solis

Secretary Hilda Solis is the Secretary of Labor under the Obama Administration. Prior to her appointment, Solis represented the 32nd Congressional District in California, where she served from 2001 through 2009. Solis is a recognized leader on clean energy jobs and environmental justice. In 1999, her California environmental legislation was the first of its kind in the nation to become law; and in 2000, she was the first woman to receive the John F. Kennedy Profile in Courage Award. She also authored the Green Jobs Act of 2007 which provided funding for "green" collar job training for veterans, displaced workers, at risk youth, and individuals in families under 200 percent of the federal poverty line.

Barton J. Taylor, M.P.A.

Barton J. Taylor is the Director of Organization Services for the Chicago Public Schools, where he manages multiple teams for Business Services, E-Rate, Organization Change Management and Project Management. He is the President of the National Urban League Young Professionals.

Valerie R. Wilson, Ph.D.
Dr. Valerie Rawlston Wilson is an economist
and Vice President of Research at the National
Urban League Policy Institute where she is
responsible for planning and directing the
research agenda. She has written on topics in
the fields of labor economics, economics of
higher education, poverty and racial inequality.
She also serves on the National Urban League
President's Council of Economic Advisors.

Index of Authors & Articles

In 1987, the National Urban League began publishing *The State of Black America* in a smaller, typeset format. By so doing, it became easier to catalog and archive the various essays by author and article.

The 2010 edition of *The State of Black America* is the sixteenth to contain an Index of the Authors and Articles that have appeared since 1987. The articles have been divided by topic and are listed in the alphabetical order of their authors' names.

Reprints of the articles catalogued herein are available through the National Urban League Policy Institute, 1101 Connecticut Avenue, NW, Suite 810, Washington, DC 20036, 202-898-1604.

Johns, David J., "Re-imagining Black Masculine Identity: An Investigation of the 'Problem' Surrounding the Construction of Black Masculinity in America," 2007, pp. 59-73.

Lanier, James R., "The Empowerment Movement and the Black Male," 2004, pp. 143–148.

———, "The National Urban League's Commission on the Black Male: Renewal, Revival and Resurrection Feasibility and Strategic Planning Study," 2005, pp. 107–109.

Morial, Marc H., "Empowering Black Males to Reach Their Full Potential," 2007, pp. 13-15.

Reed, James, and Aaron Thomas, The National Urban League: The National Urban League: Empowering Black Males to Reach Their Full Potential, 2007, pp. 217-218.

Rodgers III, William, M., "Why Should African Americans Care About Macroeconomic Policy," 2007, pp. 89-103.

Wilson, Valerie Rawlston, "On Equal Ground: Causes and Solutions for Lower College Completion Rates Among Black Males," 2007, pp. 123-135.

BUSINESS

Emerson, Melinda F., "Five Things You Must Have to Run a Successful Business," 2004, pp. 153–156.

Glasgow, Douglas G., "The Black Underclass in Perspective," 1987, pp. 129–144.

Henderson, Lenneal J., "Empowerment through Enterprise: African-American Business Development," 1993, pp. 91–108.

Price, Hugh B., "Beacons in a New Millennium: Reflections on 21st-Century Leaders and Leadership," 2000, pp. 13–39.

Tidwell, Billy J., "Black Wealth: Facts and Fiction," 1988, pp. 193–210.

Turner, Mark D., "Escaping the 'Ghetto' of Subcontracting," 2006, pp. 117–131.

Walker, Juliet E.K., "The Future of Black Business in America: Can It Get Out of the Box?," 2000, pp. 199–226.

CHILDREN AND YOUTH

Bell, William C., "How are the Children? Foster Care and African-American Boys," 2007, pp. 151-157.

Comer, James P., "Leave No Child Behind: Preparing Today's Youth for Tomorrow's World," 2005, pp.75–84.

Cox, Kenya L. Covington, "The Childcare Imbalance: Impact on Working Opportunities for Poor Mothers," 2003, pp. 197–224d.

Edelman, Marian Wright, "The State of Our Children," 2006, pp. 133–141.

———, "Losing Our Children in America's Cradle to Prison Pipeline," 2007, pp. 219-227.

Fulbright-Anderson, Karen, "Developing Our Youth: What Works," 1996, pp. 127–143.

Hare, Bruce R., "Black Youth at Risk," 1988, pp. 81–93.

Howard, Jeff P., "The Third Movement: Developing Black Children for the 21st Century," 1993, pp. 11–34.

Knaus, Christopher B., "Still Segregated, Still Unequal: Analyzing the Impact of No Child Left Behind on African-American Students," 2007, pp. 105-121.

McMurray, Georgia L. "Those of Broader Vision: An African-American Perspective on Teenage Pregnancy and Parenting," 1990, pp. 195–211.

Moore, Evelyn K., "The Call: Universal Child Care," 1996, pp. 219–244.

Scott, Kimberly A., "A Case Study: African-American Girls and Their Families," 2003, pp. 181–195.

Williams, Terry M., and William Kornblum, "A Portrait of Youth: Coming of Age in Harlem Public Housing," 1991, pp. 187–207.

CIVIC ENGAGEMENT

Alton, Kimberley, "The State of Civil Rights 2008," 2008, pp. 157–161.

Campbell, Melanie L., "Election Reform: Protecting Our Vote from the Enemy That Never Sleeps," 2008, pp. 149-156.

Lindsay, Tiffany, "Weaving the Fabric: The Political Activism of Young African- American Women," 2008, pp. 187–192.

CIVIL RIGHTS

Alton, Kimberley, "The State of Civil Rights 2008," 2008, pp. 157–161.

Archer, Dennis W., "Security Must Never Trump Liberty," 2004, pp. 139–142.

Burnham, David, "The Fog of War," 2005, pp. 123-127.

Campbell, Melanie L., "Election Reform: Protecting Our Vote from the Enemy That Never Sleeps," 2008, pp. 149-156.

Grant, Gwen, "The Fullness of Time for a More Perfect Union: The Movement Continues," 2009, pp. 171-177.

Jones, Nathaniel R., "The State of Civil Rights," 2006, pp. 165–170.

———, "Did I Ever" 2009, pp. 213-219.

Ogletree, Jr., Charles J., "Brown at 50: Considering the Continuing Legal Struggle for Racial Justice," 2004, pp. 81–96.

Shaw, Theodore M., "The State of Civil Rights," 2007, pp. 173-183.

CRIMINAL JUSTICE

Curry, George E., "Racial Disparities Drive Prison Boom," 2006, pp. 171–187.

Drucker, Ernest M., "The Impact of Mass Incarceration on Public Health in Black Communities," 2003, pp. 151–168.

Edelman, Marian Wright, "Losing Our Children in America's Cradle to Prison Pipeline," 2007, pp. 219-227.

Lanier, James R., "The Harmful Impact of the Criminal Justice System and War on Drugs on the African-American Family," 2003, pp. 169–179.

DIVERSITY

Bell, Derrick, "The Elusive Quest for Racial Justice: The Chronicle of the Constitutional Contradiction," 1991, pp. 9–23.

Cobbs, Price M., "Critical Perspectives on the Psychology of Race," 1988, pp. 61–70.

———, "Valuing Diversity: The Myth and the Challenge," 1989, pp. 151–159.

Darity, William Jr., "History, Discrimination and Racial Inequality," 1999, pp. 153–166.

Jones, Stephanie J., "Sunday Morning Apartheid: A Diversity Study of the Sunday Morning Talk Shows," 2006, pp. 189-228.

Watson, Bernard C., "The Demographic Revolution: Diversity in 21st-Century America," 1992, pp. 31–59.

Wiley, Maya, "Hurricane Katrina Exposed the Face of Diversity," 2006, pp. 143–153.

DRUG TRADE

Lanier, James R., "The Harmful Impact of the Criminal Justice System and War on Drugs on the African-American Family," 2003, pp. 169–179.

ECONOMICS

Alexis, Marcus and Geraldine R. Henderson, "The Economic Base of African-American Communities: A Study of Consumption Patterns," 1994, pp. 51–82.

Anderson, Bernard, "Lessons Learned from the Economic Crisis: Job Creation and Economy Recovery," 2010, pp. 60-65.

Bradford, William, "Black Family Wealth in the United States," 2000, pp. 103-145.

———, "Money Matters: Lending Discrimination in African-American Communities," 1993, pp. 109–134.

Burbridge, Lynn C., "Toward Economic Self-Sufficiency: Independence Without Poverty," 1993, pp. 71–90.

Edwards, Harry, "Playoffs and Payoffs: The African-American Athlete as an Institutional Resource," 1994, pp. 85–111.

Graves Jr., Earl, "Wealth for Life," 2009, pp. 165-170.

Hamilton, Darrick, "The Racial Composition of American Jobs," 2006, pp. 77-115.

Harris, Andrea, "The Subprime Wipeout: Unsustainable Loans Erase Gains Made by African-American Women," 2008, pp. 125-133.

Henderson, Lenneal J., "Blacks, Budgets, and Taxes: Assessing the Impact of Budget Deficit Reduction and Tax Reform on Blacks," 1987, pp. 75–95.

———, "Budget and Tax Strategy: Implications for Blacks," 1990, pp. 53–71.

———, "Public Investment for Public Good: Needs, Benefits, and Financing Options," 1992, pp. 213–229.

Herman, Alexis, "African-American Women and Work: Still a Tale of Two Cities," 2008, pp. 109-113.

Holzer, Harry J., "Reconnecting Young Black Men: What Policies Would Help," 2007, pp. 75-87.

Jeffries, John M., and Richard L. Schaffer, "Changes in Economy and Labor Market Status of Black Americans," 1996, pp. 12-77.

Jones, Stephanie J., "The Subprime Meltdown: Disarming the 'Weapons of Mass Deception,'" 2009, pp. 157-164.

Malveaux, Julianne, "Shouldering the Third Burden: The Status of African-American Women," 2008, pp. 75-81.

———, "The Parity Imperative: Civil Rights, Economic Justice, and the New American Dilemma," 1992, pp. 281–303.

Mensah, Lisa, "Putting Homeownership Back Within Our Reach," 2008, pp. 135-142.

Morial, Marc H. and Marvin Owens, "The National Urban League Economic Empowerment Initiative," 2005, pp. 111-113.

Myers, Jr., Samuel L., "African-American Economic Well-Being During the Boom and Bust," 2004, pp. 53–80.

National Urban League, The National Urban League's Homebuyer's Bill of Rights, 2008, pp. 143-147.

National Urban League Research Staff, "African Americans in Profile: Selected Demographic, Social and Economic Data," 1992, pp. 309–325.

———, "The Economic Status of African Americans During the Reagan-Bush Era Withered Opportunities, Limited Outcomes, and Uncertain Outlook," 1993, pp. 135–200.

———, "The Economic Status of African Americans: Limited Ownership and Persistent Inequality," 1992, pp. 61–117.

———, "The Economic Status of African Americans: 'Permanent' Poverty and Inequality," 1991, pp. 25–75.

———, "Economic Status of Black Americans During the 1980s: A Decade of Limited Progress," 1990, pp. 25–52.

———, "Economic Status of Black Americans," 1989, pp. 9–39.

———, "Economic Status of Black 1987," 1988, pp. 129–152.

———, "Economic Status of Blacks 1986," 1987, pp. 49–73.

Reuben, Lucy J., "Make Room for the New 'She'EOs: An Analysis of Businesses Owned by Black Females," 2008, pp. 115-124.

Richardson, Cy, "What Must Be Done: The Case for More Homeownership and Financial Education Counseling," 2009, pp. 145-155.

Rodgers III, William, M., "Why Should African Americans Care About Macroeconomic Policy," 2007, pp. 89-103.

Shapiro, Thomas M., "The Racial Wealth Gap," 2005, pp. 41–48.

Spriggs, William, "Nothing Trickled Down: Why Reaganomics Failed America," 2009, pp. 123-133.

Taylor, Robert D., "Wealth Creation: The Next Leadership Challenge," 2005, pp. 119–122.

Thompson, J. Phil, "The Coming Green Economy," 2009, pp. 135-142

Tidwell, Billy J., "Economic Costs of American Racism," 1991, pp. 219–232.

Turner, Mark D., "Escaping the 'Ghetto' of Subcontracting," 2006, pp. 117-131.

Watkins, Celeste, "The Socio-Economic Divide Among Black Americans Under 35," 2001, pp. 67-85.

Webb, Michael B., "Programs for Progress and Empowerment: The Urban League's National Education Initiative," 1993, pp. 203-216.

EDUCATION
Allen, Walter R., "The Struggle Continues: Race, Equity and Affirmative Action in U.S. Higher Education," 2001, pp. 87-100.

Bailey, Deirdre, "School Choice: The Option of Success," 2001, pp. 101-114.

Bradford, William D., "Dollars for Deeds: Prospects and Prescriptions for African-American Financial Institutions," 1994, pp. 31–50.

Cole, Johnnetta Betsch, "The Triumphs and Challenges of Historically Black Colleges and Universities," 2008, pp. 99-107.

Comer, James P., Norris Haynes, and Muriel Hamilton-Leel, "School Power: A Model for Improving Black Student Achievement," 1990, pp. 225–238.

———"Leave No Child Behind: Preparing Today's Youth for Tomorrow's World," 2005, pp. 75–84.

Dilworth, Mary E. "Historically Black Colleges and Universities: Taking Care of Home," 1994, pp. 127–151.

Duncan, Arne, "The Path to Success for African Americans," 2010, pp. 92-96.

Edelman, Marian Wright, "Black Children in America," 1989, pp. 63–76.

Fattah, Chaka, "Needed: Equality in Education," 2009, pp. 57-60

Freeman, Dr. Kimberly Edelin, "African-American Men and Women in Higher Education: 'Filling the Glass' in the New Millennium," 2000, pp. 61–90.

Gordon, Edmund W., "The State of Education in Black America," 2004, pp. 97–113.

Guinier, Prof. Lani, "Confirmative Action in a Multiracial Democracy," 2000, pp. 333–364.

Hanson, Renee R., "A Pathway to School Readiness: The Impact of Family on Early Childhood Education," 2008, pp. 89-98.

Jackson, John, "From Miracle to Movement: Mandating a National Opportunity to Learn, 2009, pp. 61-70.

Journal of Blacks in Higher Education (reprint), "The 'Acting White' Myth," 2005, pp.115–117.

Knaus, Christopher B., "Still Segregated, Still Unequal: Analyzing the Impact of No Child Left Behind on African American Students," 2007, pp. 105-121.

McBay, Shirley M. "The Condition of African American Education: Changes and Challenges," 1992, pp. 141–156.

McKenzie, Floretta Dukes with Patricia Evans, "Education Strategies for the 90s," 1991, pp. 95–109.

Robinson, Sharon P., "Taking Charge: An Approach to Making the Educational Problems of Blacks Comprehensible and Manageable," 1987, pp. 31–47.

Rose, Dr. Stephanie Bell, "African-American High Achievers: Developing Talented Leaders," 2000, pp. 41–60.

Ross, Ronald O., "Gaps, Traps and Lies: African-American Students and Test Scores," 2004, pp. 157–161.

Smith, Hal, "The Questions Before Us: Opportunity, Education and Equity," 2009, pp. 45-55.

Sudarkasa, Niara, "Black Enrollment in Higher Education: The Unfulfilled Promise of Equality," 1988, pp. 7–22.

Watson, Bernard C., with Fasaha M. Traylor, "Tomorrow's Teachers: Who Will They Be, What Will They Know?" 1988, pp. 23–37.

Willie, Charles V., "The Future of School Desegregation," 1987, pp. 37–47.

Wilson, Reginald, "Black Higher Education: Crisis and Promise," 1989, pp. 121–135.

Wilson, Valerie Rawlston, "On Equal Ground: Causes and Solutions for Lower College Completion Rates Among Black Males," 2007, pp. 123-135.

Wirschem, David, "Community Mobilization for Education in Rochester, New York: A Case Study," 1991, pp. 243-248.

EMERGING IDEAS
Huggins, Sheryl, "The Rules of the Game," 2001, pp. 65-66.

EMPLOYMENT
Anderson, Bernard E., "The Black Worker: Continuing Quest for Economic Parity, 2002, pp. 51-67.

Coulter, Patricia, "Small Business Growth = Job Growth," 2010, pp. 118-124.

Darity, William M., Jr., and Samuel L.Myers, Jr., "Racial Earnings Inequality into the 21st Century," 1992, pp. 119–139.

Dodd, Christopher, "Infrastructure as a Job Creation Mechanism," 2009, pp. 101-108.

Hamilton, Darrick, "The Racial Composition of American Jobs," 2006, pp. 77–115.

Hammond, Theresa A., "African Americans in White-Collar Professions," 2002, pp. 109–121.

Herman, Alexis, "African-American Women and Work: Still a Tale of Two Cities," 2008, pp. 109-113.

Nightingale, Demetra S., "Intermediaries in the Workforce Development Systsem," 2010, pp. 84-91.

Reuben, Lucy J., "Make Room for the New 'She'EOs: An Analysis of Businesses Owned by Black Females," 2008, pp. 115-124.

Rodgers, William, "Why Reduce African-American Male Unemployment?," 2009, pp. 109-121.

Solis, Hilda, "Creating Good Jobs for Everyone," 2010, pp. 66-72.

Taylor, Barton, "Opening New Doors Through Volunteerism," 2010, pp. 126-131.

Thomas, R. Roosevelt, Jr., "Managing Employee Diversity: An Assessment," 1991, pp. 145–154.

Tidwell, Billy, J., "Parity Progress and Prospects: Racial Inequalities in Economic

Well-being," 2000, pp. 287–316.

———, "African Americans and the 21st- Century Labor Market: Improving the Fit," 1993, pp. 35–57.

———, "The Unemployment Experience of African Americans: Some Important Correlates and Consequences," 1990, pp. 213–223.

———, "A Profile of the Black Unemployed," 1987, pp. 223–237.

EQUALITY
Raines, Franklin D., "What Equality Would Look Like: Reflections on the Past, Present and Future, 2002, pp. 13-27.

EQUALITY INDEX
Global Insight, Inc., The National Urban League Equality Index, 2004, pp. 15-34.

———, The National Urban League Equality Index, 2005, pp. 15-40.

———, The National Urban League Equality Index, 2010, pp. 18-39.

Thompson, Rondel and Sophia Parker of Global Insight, Inc., The National Urban League Equality Index, 2006, pp. 13-60.

Thompson, Rondel and Sophia Parker of Global Insight, Inc., The National Urban League Equality Index, 2007 pp. 17-58.

Wilson, Valerie Rawlston, The National Urban League 2008 Equality Index: Analysis, 2008, pp. 15-24.

Wilson, Valerie Rawlston, The National Urban League 2008 Equality Index, 2009, pp. 15-24.

FAMILIES
Battle, Juan, Cathy J. Cohen, Angelique Harris, and Beth E. Richie, "We Are Family: Embracing Our Lesbian, Gay, Bisexual, and Transgender (LGBT) Family Members," 2003, pp. 93-106.

Billingsley, Andrew, "Black Families in a Changing Society," 1987, pp. 97–111.

———, "Understanding African-American Family Diversity," 1990, pp. 85–108.

Cox, Kenya L. Covington, "The Childcare Imbalance: Impact on Working Opportunities for Poor Mothers," 2003, pp. 197-224d.

Drucker, Ernest M., "The Impact of Mass Incarceration on Public Health in Black Communities," 2003, pp. 151-168.

Dyson, Eric Michael, "Sexual Fault Lines: Robbing the Love Between Us," 2007, pp. 229-237.

Hanson, Renee R., "A Pathway to School Readiness: The Impact of Family on Early Childhood Education," 2008, pp. 89-98.

Hill, Robert B., "Critical Issues for Black Families by the Year 2000," 1989, pp. 41–61.

———, "The Strengths of Black Families' Revisited," 2003, pp. 107-149.

Ivory, Steven, "Universal Fatherhood: Black Men Sharing the Load," 2007, pp. 243-247.

Rawlston, Valerie A., "The Impact of Social Security on Child Poverty," 2000, pp. 317–331.

Scott, Kimberly A., "A Case Study: African-American Girls and Their Families," 2003, pp. 181-195.

Shapiro, Thomas M., "The Racial Wealth Gap," 2005, pp. 41-48.

Stafford, Walter, Angela Dews, Melissa Mendez, and Diana Salas, "Race, Gender and Welfare Reform: The Need for Targeted Support," 2003, pp. 41-92.

Stockard (Jr.), Russell L. and M. Belinda Tucker, "Young African-American Men and Women: Separate Paths?," 2001, pp. 143-159.

Teele, James E., "E. Franklin Frazier: The Man and His Intellectual Legacy," 2003, pp. 29-40.

Thompson, Dr. Linda S. and Georgene Butler, "The Role of the Black Family in Promoting Healthy Child Development," 2000, pp. 227–241.

West, Carolyn M., "Feminism is a Black Thing"?: Feminist Contribution to Black Family Life, 2003, pp. 13-27.

Willie, Charles V. "The Black Family: Striving Toward Freedom," 1988, pp. 71–80.

FOREWORD
Height, Dorothy I., "Awakenings," 2008, pp. 9-10.

Obama, Barack, Foreword, 2007, pp. 9-12.

King III, Martin Luther, Foreword, 2009, pp. 9-10.

FROM THE PRESIDENT'S DESK
Morial, Marc H., "The State of Black America: The Complexity of Black Progress," 2004, pp. 11-14.

———, "The State of Black America: Prescriptions for Change," 2005, pp. 11–14.

———, "The National Urban League Opportunity Compact," 2006, pp. 9–11.

———, "Empowering Black Males to Reach Their Full Potential," 2007,pp. 13-15.

———, From the President's Desk, 2008, pp. 11-14.

———, From the President's Desk, 2009, pp. 11-13.

———, From the President's Desk, 2010, pp. 6-7.

HEALTH
Browne, Doris, "The Impact of Health Disparities in African-American Women," 2008, pp. 163-171.

Carnethon, Mercedes R., "Black Male Life Expectancy in the United States: A Multi-level Exploration of Causes," 2007, pp. 137-150.

Cooper, Maudine R., "The Invisibility Blues' of Black Women in America," 2008, pp. 83-87.

Christmas, June Jackson, "The Health of African Americans: Progress Toward Healthy People 2000," 1996, pp. 95–126.

Gaskin, Darrell, "Improving African Americans Access to Quality Healthcare," 2009, pp. 73-86.

Hamilton, Darrick, Goldsmith, Arthur H., and Darity, William, "An Alternative 'Public Option'," 2010, pp. 98-110.

Leffall, LaSalle D., Jr., "Health Status of Black Americans," 1990, pp. 121–142.

McAlpine, Robert, "Toward Development of a National Drug Control Strategy," 1991, pp. 233–241.

Morris, Eboni D., "By the Numbers: Uninsured African-American Women," 2008, pp. 173-177.

——— and Lisa Bland Malone, "Healthy Housing," 2009, pp. 87-98.

Nobles, Wade W., and Lawford L. Goddard, "Drugs in the African-American Community: A Clear and Present Danger," 1989, pp. 161–181.

Primm, Annelle and Marisela B. Gomez, "The Impact of Mental Health on Chronic Disease," 2005, pp. 63–73.

Primm, Beny J., "AIDS: A Special Report," 1987, pp. 159–166.

———, "Drug Use: Special Implications for Black America," 1987, pp. 145–158.

Smedley, Brian D., "Race, Poverty, and Healthcare Disparities," 2006, pp. 155–164.

Williams, David R., "Health and the Quality of Life Among African Americans," 2004, pp. 115-138.

HOUSING

Calmore, John O., "To Make Wrong Right: The Necessary and Proper Aspirations of Fair Housing," 1989, pp. 77–109.

Clay, Phillip, "Housing Opportunity: A Dream Deferred," 1990, pp. 73–84.

Cooper, Maudine R., "The Invisibility Blues' of Black Women in America," 2008, pp. 83-87.

Freeman, Lance, "Black Homeownership: A Dream No Longer Deferred?," 2006, pp. 63–75.

_____, "Housing in the Post-Bubble Economy," 2010, pp. 74-83.

Harris, Andrea, "The Subprime Wipeout: Unsustainable Loans Erase Gains Made by African-American Women," 2008, pp. 125-133.

James, Angela, "Black Homeownership: Housing and Black Americans Under 35," 2001, pp. 115-129.

Jones, Stephanie J., "The Subprime Meltdown: Disarming the 'Weapons of Mass Deception,'" 2009, pp. 157-164.

Leigh, Wilhelmina A., "U.S. Housing Policy in 1996: The Outlook for Black Americans," 1996, pp. 188–218.

Morris, Eboni and Lisa Bland Malone, "Healthy Housing," 2009, pp. 87-98.

Richardson, Cy, "What Must Be Done: The Case for More Homeownership and Financial Education Counseling," 2009, pp. 145-155.

Spriggs, William, "Nothing Trickled Down: Why Reaganomics Failed America," 2009. pp. 123-133.

IN MEMORIAM

National Urban League, "William A. Bootle, Ray Charles, Margo T. Clarke, Ossie Davis, Herman C. Ewing, James Forman, Joanne Grant, Ann Kheel, Memphis Norman, Max Schmeling," 2005, pp. 139–152.

———, "Renaldo Benson, Shirley Chisholm, Johnnie Cochran, Jr., Shirley Horn, John H. Johnson, Vivian Malone Jones, Brock Peters, Richard Pryor, Bobby Short, C. Delores Tucker, August Wilson, Luther Vandross, and NUL members Clarence Lyle Barney, Jr., Manuel Augustus Romero;" 2006, pp. 279–287.

———, "Ossie Davis: Still Caught in the Dream," 2005, pp. 137–138.

———, "Ed Bradley, James Brown, Bebe Moore Campbell, Katherine Dunham, Mike Evans, Coretta Scott King, Gerald Levert, Gordon Parks, June Pointer, Lou Rawls, and Helen E. Harden," 2007, pp. 249-257.

———, "Effi Barry, Jane Bolin, Daniel A. Collins (NUL Member), Oliver Hill, Yolanda King, Calvin Lockhart, Mahlon Puryear (NUL Member), Max Roach, Eddie Robinson, William Simms (NUL Member), Darryl Stingley, and Ike Turner," 2008, pp. 205-217.

———, In Memoriam, 2009, pp. 225-241.

Jones, Stephanie J., "Rosa Parks: An Ordinary Woman, An Extraordinary Life," 2006, pp. 245–246.

MILITARY AFFAIRS

Butler, John Sibley, "African Americans and the American Military," 2002, pp. 93-107.

MUSIC

Boles, Mark A., "Breaking the 'Hip Hop' Hold: Looking Beyond the Media Hype," 2007, pp. 239-241.

Brown, David W., "Their Characteristic Music: Thoughts on Rap Music and Hip-Hop Culture," 2001, pp. 189–201.

Bynoe, Yvonne, "The Roots of Rap Music and Hip-Hop Culture: One Perspective," 2001, pp. 175–187.

OP-ED/COMMENTARY

Archer, Dennis W., "Security Must Never Trump Liberty," 2004, pp. 139–142.

Bailey, Moya, "Going in Circles: The Struggle to Diversify Popular Images of Black Women," 2008, pp. 193-196.

Bernard, Michelle, "An Ode to Black America," 2009, pp. 203-207.

Boles, Mark A., "Breaking the 'Hip Hop' Hold: Looking Beyond the Media Hype," 2007, pp. 239-241.

Burnham, David, "The Fog of War," 2005, pp. 123–127.

Cooke, Cassye, "The Game Changer: Are We Beyond What is Next to What is Now?," 2009, pp. 209-212.

Covington, Kenya L., "The Transformation of the Welfare Caseload," 2004, pp. 149–152.

Dyson, Eric Michael, "Sexual Fault Lines: Robbing the Love Between Us," 2007, pp. 229-237.

Edelman, Marian Wright, "Losing Our Children in America's Cradle to Prison Pipeline," 2007, pp. 219-227.

Emerson, Melinda F., "Five Things You Must Have to Run a Successful Business," 2004, pp. 153–156.

Ivory, Steven, "Universal Fatherhood: Black Men Sharing the Load," 2007, pp. 243-247.

Jones, Nathaniel R., "Did I Ever? Yes I Did," 2009, pp. 213-219.

Journal of Blacks in Higher Education (reprint), "The 'Acting White' Myth," 2005, pp. 115–117.

Lanier, James R., "The Empowerment Movement and the Black Male," 2004, pp. 143–148.

Lee, Barbara, "President Obama and the CBC: Speaking with One Voice," 2009, pp. 193-197.

Lindsay, Tiffany, "Weaving the Fabric: the Political Activism of Young African-American Women," 2008, pp. 187-192.

Malveaux, Julianne, "Black Women's Hands Can Rock the World: Global Involvement and Understanding," 2008, pp. 197-202.

Ross, Ronald O., "Gaps, Traps and Lies: African-American Students and Test Scores," 2004, pp. 157–161.

Taylor, Susan L., "Black Love Under Siege," 2008 pp. 179-186.

Taylor, Robert D., "Wealth Creation: The Next Leadership Challenge," 2005, pp. 119–122.

West, Cornel, "Democracy Matters," 2005, pp. 129–132.

OVERVIEW
Morial, Marc H., "Black America's Family Matters," 2003, pp. 9-12.

Price, Hugh B., "Still Worth Fighting For: America After 9/11," 2002, pp. 9-11.

POLITICS
Alton, Kimberley, "The State of Civil Rights 2008," 2008, pp. 157-161.

Campbell, Melanie L., "Election Reform: Protecting Our Vote from the Enemy Who Never Sleeps," 2008, pp. 149-156.

Coleman, Henry A., "Interagency and Intergovernmental Coordination: New Demands for Domestic Policy Initiatives," 1992, pp. 249–263.

Hamilton, Charles V., "On Parity and Political Empowerment," 1989, pp. 111–120.

————, "Promoting Priorities: African-American Political Influence in the 1990s," 1993, pp. 59–69.

Henderson, Lenneal J., "Budgets, Taxes, and Politics: Options for the African-American Community," 1991, pp. 77–93.

Holden, Matthew, Jr., "The Rewards of Daring and the Ambiguity of Power: Perspectives on the Wilder Election of 1989," 1990, pp. 109–120.

Kilson, Martin L., "African Americans and American Politics 2002: The Maturation Phase," 2002, pp. 147–180.

————, "Thinking About the Black Elite's Role: Yesterday and Today," 2005, pp. 85-106.

Lee, Silas, "Who's Going to Take the Weight? African Americans and Civic Engagement in the 21st Century," 2007, pp. 185-192.

Lindsay, Tiffany, "Weaving the Fabric: The Political Activism of Young African-American Women," 2008, pp. 187-192.

McHenry, Donald F., "A Changing World Order: Implications for Black America," 1991, pp. 155–163.

Persons, Georgia A., "Blacks in State and Local Government: Progress and Constraints," 1987, pp. 167–192.

Pinderhughes, Dianne M., "Power and Progress: African-American Politics in the New Era of Diversity," 1992, pp. 265–280.

————, "The Renewal of the Voting Rights Act," 2005, pp. 49–61.

————, "Civil Rights and the Future of the American Presidency," 1988, pp. 39–60.

Price, Hugh B., "Black America's Challenge: The Re-construction of Black Civil Society," 2001, pp. 13-18.

Tidwell, Billy J., "Serving the National Interest: A Marshall Plan for America," 1992, pp. 11–30.

West, Cornel, "Democracy Matters," 2005, pp. 129–132.

Williams, Eddie N., "The Evolution of Black Political Power", 2000, pp. 91–102.

POVERTY
Cooper, Maudine R., "The Invisibility Blues' of Black Women in America," 2008, pp. 83-87.

Edelman, Marian Wright, "The State of Our Children," 2006, pp. 133–141.

PRESCRIPTIONS FOR CHANGE
National Urban League, "Prescriptions for Change," 2005, pp. 133-135.

RELATIONSHIPS
Taylor, Susan L., "Black Love Under Siege," 2008, pp. 179-186.

RELIGION
Lincoln, C. Eric, "Knowing the Black Church: What It Is and Why," 1989, pp. 137–149.

Richardson, W. Franklyn, "Mission to Mandate: Self-Development through the Black Church," 1994, pp. 113–126.

Smith, Dr. Drew, "The Evolving Political Priorities of African-American Churches: An Empirical View," 2000, pp. 171–197.

Taylor, Mark V.C., "Young Adults and Religion," 2001, pp. 161–174.

REPORTS FROM THE NATIONAL URBAN LEAGUE
Hanson, Renee, Mark McArdle, and Valerie Rawlston Wilson, "Invisible Men: The Urgent Problems of Low-Income African-American Males," 2007, pp. 209-216.

Lanier, James, "The National Urban League's Commission on the Black Male: Renewal, Revival and Resurrection Feasibility and Strategic Planning Study," 2005, pp. 107–109.

Jones, Stephanie J., "Sunday Morning Apartheid: A Diversity Study of the Sunday Morning Talk Shows" 2006, pp. 189–228.

National Urban League Policy Institute, The Opportunity Compact: A Blueprint for Economic Equality, 2008, pp. 43-74.

————, "Putting Americans Back to Work: The National Urban League's Plan for Creating Jobs" 2010, pp. 40-44.

————, "African Americans and the Green Revolution" 2010, pp. 46-59.

REPORTS
Joint Center for Political and Economic Studies, A Way Out: Creating Partners for Our Nation's Prosperity by Expanding Life Paths for Young Men of Color—Final Report of the Dellums Commission, 2007, pp. 193-207.

Reed, James and Aaron Thomas, The National Urban League: Empowering Black Males to Meet Their Full Potential, 2007, pp. 217-218.

SEXUAL IDENTITY
Bailey, Moya, "Going in Circles: The Struggle to Diversify Popular Images of Black Women," 2008 pp. 193-196.

Battle, Juan, Cathy J. Cohen, Angelique Harris, and Beth E. Richie, "We Are Family: Embracing Our Lesbian, Gay, Bisexual, and Transgender (LGBT) Family Members," 2003, pp. 93-106.

Taylor, Susan L., "Black Love Under Siege," 2008, pp. 179-186.

SOCIOLOGY
Cooper, Maudine R., "The Invisibility Blues' of Black Women in America," 2008, pp. 83-87.

Taylor, Susan L., "Black Love Under Siege," 2008, pp. 179-186.

Teele, James E., "E. Franklin Frazier: The Man and His Intellectual Legacy," 2003, pp. 29-40.

SPECIAL SECTION: BLACK WOMEN'S HEALTH
Browne, Doris, "The Impact of Health Disparities in African-American Women," 2008, pp. 163-171.

Morris, Eboni D., "By the Numbers: Uninsured African-American Women," 2008, pp. 173-177.

SPECIAL SECTION: KATRINA AND BEYOND
Brazile, Donna L., "New Orleans: Next Steps on the Road to Recovery," 2006, pp. 233–237.

Morial, Marc H., "New Orleans Revisited," 2006, pp. 229–232.

National Urban League, "The National Urban League Katrina Bill of Rights," 2006, pp. 239–243.

SURVEYS
The National Urban League Survey, 2004, pp. 35-51.

Stafford, Walter S., "The National Urban League Survey: Black America's Under-35 Generation," 2001, pp. 19-63.

————, "The New York Urban League Survey: Black New York— On Edge, But Optimistic," 2001, pp. 203-219.

TECHNOLOGY
Dreyfuss, Joel, "Black Americans and the Internet: The Technological Imperative," 2001, pp. 131-141.

Ramsey, Rey, "Broadband Matters to All of Us," 2010, pp. 112-116.

Wilson Ernest J., III, "Technological Convergence, Media Ownership and Content Diversity," 2000, pp. 147–170.

URBAN AFFAIRS
Allen, Antoine, and Leland Ware, "The Geography of Discrimination: Hypersegregation, Isolation and Fragmentation Within the African-American Community," 2002, pp. 69–92.

Bates, Timothy, "The Paradox of Urban Poverty," 1996, pp. 144–163.

Bell, Carl C., with Esther J. Jenkins, "Preventing Black Homicide," 1990, pp. 143–155.

Bryant Solomon, Barbara, "Social Welfare Reform," 1987, pp. 113–127.

Brown, Lee P., "Crime in the Black Community," 1988, pp. 95–113.

Bullard, Robert D. "Urban Infrastructure: Social, Environmental, and Health Risks to African Americans," 1992, pp.183–196.

Chambers, Julius L., "The Law and Black Americans: Retreat from Civil Rights," 1987, pp. 15–30.

————, "Black Americans and the Courts: Has the Clock Been Turned Back Permanently?" 1990, pp. 9–24.

Edelin, Ramona H., "Toward an African-American Agenda: An Inward Look," 1990, pp. 173–183.

Fair, T. Willard, "Coordinated Community Empowerment: Experiences of the Urban League of Greater Miami," 1993, pp. 217–233.

Gray, Sandra T., "Public-Private Partnerships: Prospects for America... Promise for African Americans," 1992, pp. 231–247.

Harris, David, " 'Driving While Black' and Other African-American Crimes: The Continuing Relevance of Race to American Criminal Justice," 2000, pp. 259–285.

Henderson, Lenneal J., "African Americans in the Urban Milieu: Conditions, Trends, and Development Needs," 1994, pp. 11–29.

Hill, Robert B., "Urban Redevelopment: Developing Effective Targeting Strategies," 1992, pp. 197–211.

Jones, Dionne J., with Greg Harrison of the National Urban League Research Department, "Fast Facts: Comparative Views of African-American Status and Progress," 1994, pp. 213–236.

Jones, Shirley J., "Silent Suffering: The Plight of Rural Black America," 1994, pp.171–188.

Massey, Walter E. "Science, Technology, and Human Resources: Preparing for the 21st Century," 1992, pp. 157–169.

Mendez, Jr. Garry A., "Crime Is Not a Part of Our Black Heritage: A Theoretical Essay," 1988, pp. 211–216.

Miller, Warren F., Jr., "Developing Untapped Talent: A National Call for African-American Technologists," 1991, pp. 111–127.

Murray, Sylvester, "Clear and Present Danger: The Decay of America's Physical Infrastructure," 1992, pp. 171–182.

Pemberton, Gayle, "It's the Thing That Counts, Or Reflections on the Legacy of W.E.B. Du Bois," 1991, pp. 129–143.

Pinderhughes, Dianne M., "The Case of African-Americans in the Persian Gulf: The Intersection of American Foreign and Military Policy with Domestic Employment Policy in the United States," 1991, pp. 165–186.

Robinson, Gene S. "Television Advertising and Its Impact on Black America," 1990, pp. 157–171.

Sawyers, Dr. Andrew and Dr. Lenneal Henderson, "Race, Space and Justice: Cities and Growth in the 21st Century," 2000, pp. 243–258.

Schneider, Alvin J., "Blacks in the Military: The Victory and the Challenge," 1988, pp. 115–128.

Smedley, Brian, "Race, Poverty, and Healthcare Disparities," 2006, pp. 155–164.

Stafford, Walter, Angela Dews, Melissa Mendez, and Diana Salas, "Race, Gender and Welfare Reform: The Need for Targeted Support," 2003, pp. 41–92.

Stewart, James B., "Developing Black and Latino Survival Strategies: The Future of Urban Areas," 1996, pp. 164–187.

Stone, Christopher E., "Crime and Justice in Black America," 1996, pp. 78–94.

Tidwell, Billy J., with Monica B. Kuumba, Dionne J. Jones, and Betty C. Watson, "Fast Facts: African Americans in the 1990s," 1993, pp. 243–265.

Wallace-Benjamin, Joan, "Organizing African-American Self-Development: The Role of Community-Based Organizations," 1994, pp. 189–205.

Walters, Ronald, "Serving the People: African-American Leadership and the Challenge of Empowerment," 1994, pp. 153–170.

Allen, Antoine, and Leland Ware, "The Geography of Discrimination: Hypersegregation, Isolation and Fragmentation Within the African-American Community," 2002, pp. 69–92.

Wiley, Maya, "Hurricane Katrina Exposed the Face of Poverty," 2006, pp. 143–153.

WELFARE

Bergeron, Suzanne, and William E. Spriggs, "Welfare Reform and Black America," 2002, pp. 29–50.

Cooper, Maudine R., "The Invisibility Blues' of Black Women in America," 2008, pp. 83-87.

Covington, Kenya L., "The Transformation of the Welfare Caseload," 2004, pp. 149–152.

Spriggs, William E., and Suzanne Bergeron, "Welfare Reform and Black America," 2002, pp. 29–50.

Stafford, Walter, Angela Dews, Melissa Mendez, and Diana Salas, "Race, Gender and Welfare Reform: The Need for Targeted Support," 2003, pp. 41-92.

WOMEN'S ISSUES

Bailey, Moya, "Going in Circles: The Struggle to Diversify Popular Images of Black Women," 2008, pp. 193-196.

Browne, Doris, "The Impact of Health Disparities in African-American Women," 2008, pp. 163-171.

Cooper, Maudine R., "The Invisibility Blues' of Black Women in America," 2008, pp. 83-87.

Harris, Andrea, "The Subprime Wipeout: Unsustainable Loans Erase Gains Made by African-American Women," 2008, pp. 125-133.

Herman, Alexis, "African-American Women and Work: Still a Tale of Two Cities," 2008, pp. 109-113.

Lindsay, Tiffany, "Weaving the Fabric: The Political Activism of Young African-American Women," 2008, pp. 187–192.

Malveaux, Julianne, "Black Women's Hands Can Rock the World: Global Involvement and Understanding," 2008, pp. 197-202.

————, "Shouldering the Third Burden: The Status of African-American Women," 2008, pp. 75-81.

Mensah, Lisa, "Putting Homeownership Back Within Our Reach," 2008, pp. 135-142.

Morris, Eboni D., "By the Numbers: Uninsured African-American Women," 2008, pp. 173-177.

Reuben, Lucy J., "Make Room for the New 'She'EOs: An Analysis of Businesses Owned by Black Females," 2008, pp. 115-124.

Stafford, Walter, Angela Dews, Melissa Mendez, and Diana Salas, "Race, Gender and Welfare Reform: The Need for Targeted Support," 2003, pp. 41–92.

Taylor, Susan L., "Black Love Under Siege," 2008, pp. 179-186.

West, Carolyn M., "Feminism is a Black Thing?": Feminist Contribution to Black Family Life, 2003, pp. 13–27.

WORLD AFFAIRS

Malveaux, Julianne, "Black Women's Hands Can Rock the World: Global Involvement and Understanding," 2008, pp. 197-202.

National Urban League Board of Trustees

National Urban League Executive Staff

EXECUTIVE TEAM

President & CEO
Marc H. Morial

Senior Vice President
Marketing & Communications
Rhonda Spears Bell

Senior Vice President
Programs
Donald E. Bowen

Senior Vice President
Innovation
& Chief Counselor to the President
Patrick Gusman

Senior Vice President
Human Resources
& Chief Talent Officer
Wanda H. Jackson

Executive Director
Policy Institute
Stephanie J. Jones

Senior Vice President
Affiliate Services
Herman L. Lessard, Jr.

Executive Director
Centennial Commission
S. Annelle Lewis

Senior Vice President
Development
Dennis Serrette

Senior Vice President
Finance & Operations
Paul Wycisk

POLICY INSTITUTE STAFF

Executive Director
Stephanie J. Jones

Vice President & Chief of Staff
Lisa Bland Malone

Vice President of Research
Valerie Rawlston Wilson

Senior Legislative Director
Suzanne M. Bergeron

Research Analyst
Madura Wijewardena

Assistant
Clarissa McKithen

Office Manager
Gail Thomas

Roster of National Urban League Affiliates

AKRON, OHIO
Akron Community Service Center
and Urban League

ALEXANDRIA, VIRGINIA
Northern Virginia Urban League

ANCHORAGE, ALASKA
Urban League of Anchorage-Alaska

ALTON, ILLINOIS
Madison County Urban League

ANDERSON, INDIANA
Urban League of Madison County, Inc.

ATLANTA, GEORGIA
Atlanta Urban League

AURORA, ILLINOIS
Quad County Urban League

AUSTIN, TEXAS
Austin Area Urban League

BALTIMORE, MARYLAND
Greater Baltimore Urban League

BATTLE CREEK, MICHIGAN
Southwestern Michigan Urban League

BINGHAMTON, NEW YORK
Broome County Urban League

BIRMINGHAM, ALABAMA
Birmingham Urban League

BOSTON, MASSACHUSETTS
Urban League of Eastern Massachusetts

BUFFALO, NEW YORK
Buffalo Urban League

CANTON, OHIO
Greater Stark County
Urban League, Inc.

**CHARLESTON,
SOUTH CAROLINA**
Charleston Trident Urban League

**CHARLOTTE,
NORTH CAROLINA**
Urban League of Central Carolinas, Inc.

CHATTANOOGA, TENNESSEE
Urban League Greater
Chattanooga, Inc.

CHICAGO, ILLINOIS
Chicago Urban League

CINCINNATI, OHIO
Urban League of Greater Cincinnati

CLEVELAND, OHIO
Urban League of Greater Cleveland

**COLORADO SPRINGS,
COLORADO**
Urban League of Pikes Peak Region

**COLUMBIA,
SOUTH CAROLINA**
Columbia Urban League

COLUMBUS, GEORGIA
Urban League of Greater Columbus, Inc.

COLUMBUS, OHIO
Columbus Urban League

DALLAS, TEXAS
Urban League of Greater Dallas and
North Central Texas

DAYTON, OHIO
Dayton Urban League

DENVER, COLORADO
Urban League of Metropolitan Denver

DETROIT, MICHIGAN
Urban League of Detroit
and Southeastern Michigan

ELIZABETH, NEW JERSEY
Urban League of Union County

ELYRIA, OHIO
Lorain County Urban League

ENGLEWOOD, NEW JERSEY
Urban League for Bergen County

FARRELL, PENNSYLVANIA
Urban League of Shenango Valley

FLINT, MICHIGAN
Urban League of Flint

FORT LAUDERDALE, FLORIDA
Urban League of Broward County

FORT WAYNE, INDIANA
Fort Wayne Urban League

GARY, INDIANA
Urban League of
Northwest Indiana, Inc.

GRAND RAPIDS, MICHIGAN
Grand Rapids Urban League

**GREENVILLE,
SOUTH CAROLINA**
The Urban League of the Upstate

HARTFORD, CONNECTICUT
Urban League of Greater Hartford

HOUSTON, TEXAS
Houston Area Urban League

INDIANAPOLIS, INDIANA
Indianapolis Urban League

JACKSON, MISSISSIPPI
Urban League of Greater Jackson

JACKSONVILLE, FLORIDA
Jacksonville Urban League

JERSEY CITY, NEW JERSEY
Urban League of Hudson County

KANSAS CITY, MISSOURI
Urban League of Kansas City

KNOXVILLE, TENNESSEE
Knoxville Area Urban League

LANCASTER, PENNSYLVANIA
Urban League of Lancaster County

LAS VEGAS, NEVADA
Las Vegas-Clark County
Urban League

LEXINGTON, KENTUCKY
Urban League of Lexington-
Fayette County

LONG ISLAND, NEW YORK
Urban League of Long Island

LOS ANGELES, CALIFORNIA
Los Angeles Urban League

LOUISVILLE, KENTUCKY
Louisville Urban League

MADISON, WISCONSIN
Urban League of Greater Madison

MEMPHIS, TENNESSEE
Memphis Urban League

MIAMI, FLORIDA
Urban League of Greater Miami

MILWAUKEE, WISCONSIN
Milwaukee Urban League

MINNEAPOLIS, MINNESOTA
Minneapolis Urban League

MORRISTOWN, NEW JERSEY
Morris County Urban League

MUSKEGON, MICHIGAN
Urban League of Greater Muskegon

NASHVILLE, TENNESSEE
Urban League of Middle Tennessee

NEW ORLEANS, LOUISIANA
Urban League of Greater New Orleans

NEW YORK, NEW YORK
New York Urban League

NEWARK, NEW JERSEY
Urban League of Essex County

NORFOLK, VIRGINIA
Urban League of Hampton Roads

OKLAHOMA CITY,
OKLAHOMA
Urban League of Oklahoma City

OMAHA, NEBRASKA
Urban League of Nebraska

ORLANDO, FLORIDA
Metropolitan Orlando Urban League

PEORIA, ILLINOIS
Tri-County Urban League

PHILADELPHIA,
PENNSYLVANIA
Urban League of Philadelphia

PHOENIX, ARIZONA
Greater Phoenix Urban League

PITTSBURGH, PENNSYLVANIA
Urban League of Greater Pittsburgh

PORTLAND, OREGON
Urban League of Portland

PROVIDENCE, RHODE ISLAND
Urban League of Rhode Island

RACINE, WISCONSIN
Urban League of Racine & Kenosha, Inc.

RICHMOND, VIRGINIA
Urban League of Greater Richmond, Inc.

ROCHESTER, NEW YORK
Urban League of Rochester

SACRAMENTO, CALIFORNIA
Greater Sacramento Urban League

SAINT LOUIS, MISSOURI
Urban League Metropolitan St. Louis

SAINT PAUL, MINNESOTA
St. Paul Urban League

SAINT PETERSBURG, FLORIDA
Pinellas County Urban League

SAN DIEGO, CALIFORNIA
Urban League of San Diego County

SEATTLE, WASHINGTON
Urban League of Metropolitan Seattle

SPRINGFIELD, ILLINOIS
Springfield Urban League, Inc.

SPRINGFIELD,
MASSACHUSETTS
Urban League of Springfield

STAMFORD, CONNECTICUT
Urban League of Southern Connecticut

TACOMA, WASHINGTON
Tacoma Urban League

TALLAHASSEE, FLORDIA
Tallahassee Urban League

TOLEDO, OHIO
Greater Toledo Urban League

TUCSON, ARIZONA
Tucson Urban League

TULSA, OKLAHOMA
Metropolitan Tulsa Urban League

WARREN, OHIO
Greater Warren-Youngstown
Urban League

WASHINGTON, D.C.
Greater Washington Urban League

WEST PALM BEACH, FLORIDA
Urban League of Palm Beach
County, Inc.

WHITE PLAINS, NEW YORK
Urban League of Westchester County

WICHITA, KANSAS
Urban League of Kansas, Inc.

WILMINGTON, DELAWARE
Metropolitan Wilmington Urban League

WINSTON-SALEM,
NORTH CAROLINA
Winston-Salem Urban League